THE UNBELIEVER

THE UNBELIEVER

The Poetry of
Elizabeth Bishop

Robert Dale Parker

UNIVERSITY OF ILLINOIS PRESS
Urbana and Chicago

© 1988 by the Board of Trustees of the University of Illinois
Manufactured in the United States of America
C 5 4 3 2 1

This book is printed on acid-free paper.

Library of Congress Cataloging-in-Publication Data

Parker, Robert Dale, 1953-
    The unbeliever : the poetry of Elizabeth Bishop / Robert Dale
Parker.
        p.   cm.
    Bibliography: p.
    Includes index.
    ISBN 0-252-01509-6
    1. Bishop, Elizabeth, 1911-1979—Criticism and interpretation.
I. Title.
PS3503.I785Z83 1988
811'.54—dc19
                                                            87-34285
                                                            CIP

in honor of
Marlie P. Wasserman
and Carol P. McConnell

Contents

Preface

This book is a critical study of the poetry of Elizabeth Bishop. Most critics and commentators have approached Bishop's poetry with restraint, seeing it as strangely muted and reticent. Along with some other recent critics, I proceed differently. There will be no talk of "Miss Bishop" here, nor any delicate sense that we must say "Elizabeth" whenever we say "Bishop." For in addition to Bishop's famous descriptions, quiet and clear, her poems are full of confusion and wonder about things she can never make quiet or clear—about sexuality, politics, the burdens of imagination, the fate of the self.

Indeed, Bishop's poems typify and can help us understand a larger anxiety in contemporary American poetry in general: an unbelief in the self, a fear that, once having felt the vocation of *poet,* a poet still anxiously awaits the calling of any particular poem. In a lesser poet the result is mere strain, but Bishop achieves more, partly because she both senses the strain and in her best poems takes it as her tacit subject.

I see her career as dividing roughly into three stages of contention with that anxiety over poetic occasion. She begins with poems of *wish,* after which, more modestly expecting less, she resigns herself to the contrived occasion of the immediate, of what lies directly around her, and writes of *where;* until finally, as she ages and the people close to her die and she feels more and more her susceptibility to loss, where and wish both seem too transient and she turns to poems of *retrospect.* The rough scaffolding of movement from one stage to another matters less than the underlying continuity, namely, that the terms of each stage are defined by a representatively Modern and Postmodern feeling of belated entry to poethood itself, so that wish and where and retrospect all put themselves forth as unbeliever's compensations for some irretrievable immediacy of natural inspiration and vision.

My method is comparative. Occasionally, the comparisons suggest some of Bishop's sources, but comparison is fundamentally different from the ferreting out of sources. For whether we pause to think about it or not, our sense of any text comes in many ways from how we see it in relation to other texts that set up our overall system of literary norms and traditions (of what structuralist students of poetics call literary competence and convention). Throughout the book, I set contexts for Bishop's poetry through comparison with her prose and with the work of other writers, especially Dickinson, Whitman, and Robert Lowell, and also, among others, Frost, Stevens, Hemingway, and Flannery O'Connor. Though I refer to many poems, I concentrate on the major works. Chapter One discusses two poems closely and uses them to introduce the overall approach. Then a second chapter, on *wish*, studies *North & South*, Bishop's first book (including "The Unbeliever," which furnishes my title). The third chapter, on *where*, focuses on her next two books, *A Cold Spring* and *Questions of Travel*. And the fourth and final chapter, on *retrospect*, concentrates on *Geography III*, her last collection, and in particular on poems through which, late in life, Bishop looks back over the whole of her life and her career.

This book grew out of teaching. I am very grateful to my students at the University of Michigan at Ann Arbor in English 240 and 472, who convinced me that Bishop was so challenging to criticism. Though the book was first thought through at Michigan, it was written entirely at the University of Illinois at Urbana-Champaign, and I cannot thank my colleagues at Illinois enough for their encouragement and for their friendliness to a new arrival. I am grateful also to the University of Illinois Research Board for providing some extra time one semester, and to the University of Illinois Center for Advanced Study for a full semester to write. I am especially happy to have this chance to thank Richard H. Brodhead, Margaret Dickie, and Robert Weisbuch for warmly supporting this project, and to thank the publisher's readers and the colleagues and friends who graciously read and criticized part or all of the manuscript, including Ed Folsom, Diana Hume George, Kerry Larson, Brian McHale, Bruce Michelson, Cary Nelson, and Michael Stark.

I would also like to thank the University Libraries, Special Collections, Washington University in St. Louis for their assistance and for permission to quote from their Elizabeth Bishop Papers and May Swenson Papers, and to thank the Rare Books and Manuscripts department of the Vassar College Library for their assistance and for permission to quote from their Elizabeth Bishop collection. Quotations from the poems of Emily Dickinson are reprinted by permission of the publishers and trustees of Amherst College from *The Poems of Emily Dickinson*, edited by Thomas H. Johnson, Cambridge, Mass.: The Belknap Press of Harvard University Press, Copyright 1951, ©1955, 1979, 1983 by the President and Fellows of Harvard College. "Design" is quoted by permission of the publishers from *The Poetry of Robert Frost*, ed. Edward Connery Lathem, New York: Holt, Rinehart and Winston, 1969. Excerpts from "Filling Station," "The Imaginary Iceberg," "The Weed," "Songs for a Colored Singer, IV," "The Monument," "The Map," "The Unbeliever," "The Man-Moth," "The Gentleman of Shalott," "Roosters," "Chemin de Fer," "Questions of Travel," "At the Fishhouses," "Insomnia," "Brazil, January 1, 1502," "The Armadillo," "First Death in Nova Scotia," "Visits to St. Elizabeths," "The Moose," "One Art," "Crusoe in England," and "In the Waiting Room," from THE COMPLETE POEMS 1927-1979 by Elizabeth Bishop. Copyright ©1983 by Alice Helen Methfessel. Copyright ©1933, 1935, 1936, 1937, 1938, 1939, 1940, 1941, 1944, 1945, 1946, 1947, 1948, 1949, 1951, 1952, 1955, 1956, 1957, 1958, 1959, 1960, 1961, 1962, 1963, 1964, 1965, 1966, 1967, 1968, 1969, 1971, 1972, 1973, 1974, 1975, 1976 by Elizabeth Bishop. Renewal copyright ©1967, 1968, 1971, 1973, 1974, 1975, 1976, 1979 by Elizabeth Bishop. Renewal copyright ©1980 by Alice Helen Methfessel. Reprinted by permission of Farrar, Straus and Giroux, Inc. I am grateful to Alice Methfessel, Bishop's literary executor, for her kind permission to quote from unpublished materials by Bishop.

CHAPTER ONE

Bishop and the Weed
of Poetic Invention

Why the extraneous plant?

I

Why a poem?

Again and again we have asked what poems mean and how poems mean, and sometimes we have wondered why we have poems or poets at all. We have turned to this poem for that idea, which tells *what;* and we have turned to that poem for this form, which tells *how.* Either how or what is much indeed, but neither tells enough of why.

Poets think of themselves as poets before they write most of their poems and before they write virtually any poems that we read. But they know or often believe that to be a poet is no election for eternity; poets must poet, must forever reaffirm their being poets. In a world that often awards greater status to being a poet than to the poem that authorizes that being, the motive for individual poems is sometimes less an anxious struggle with the representation in the poem than it is an anxious struggle with the representation *by* the poem. The poem may mean this or be that, but it also makes the poet's very poethood, which is partially independent of what or how. Rather than the poet innocently authoring the poem, the poet's authority or authoring can grow from a wish that the poem will author the poet.

II

Readers have typically noted Elizabeth Bishop's poetry for its modesty. They praise its quiet distance, its measured and precise observation of the exterior world, and its exquisite tone of reticence, of restraint. The composite picture sounds appealingly curious—a poet quiet, distant, and delicate, heir more to the pristine Modern of Pound's *Cathay* than to the chaotic Modernism of *The Cantos,* a poet understated, cautious, and even a little finicky. Bishop's poetry is all those familiarly "feminine" things. But an increasing number of readers has begun to notice that it is also a great deal more. Often, it is terrified.

A typical Bishop poem worries its subject. "We'd rather have the iceberg than the ship, / although it meant the end of travel," she begins the early (first published in 1935) "The Imaginary Iceberg," a suspiciously confident allegory of the self-sufficiency of art and imagination. Travel is means, as it would be so often in Bishop's life and work, and iceberg—with its ominous overtones of the *Titanic*— is end. It is an end glorious enough to lose our sight for ("This is a scene a sailor'd give his eyes for"), and to be worth ending travel— or sinking—for. The iceberg floats hugely across the horizon with the lapidary finality of art itself:

> This iceberg cuts its facets from within.
> Like jewelry from a grave
> it saves itself perpetually and adorns
> only itself.

But this particular iceberg differs from the one that downed the *Titanic* because it floats in a different sea; it is imaginary. And imaginary in a fabulously ideal way: it is self-created ("cuts its facets from within"), that is, it allegorizes an impossible poetry of pure wish, a self-begotten poetry, uninherited, uninfluenced, and unanxious. It projects onto the landscape or seascape a gargantuan emblem of the child's (or poet's) pure oedipal wish to parent his or her self, or, finally, to be unparented, as natural and primeval and immortal ("from a grave / it saves itself perpetually") as the sea itself. Such an art illustrates nothing. Bishop seeks here no utilitarian poethood; her iceberg "adorns only itself." It is cold and hard, and timeless, with no history to restrain it and no future to draw it forward.

And yet, as that iceberg thus represents Bishop's early ideal of imagination and poetry, it and all its representativeness nevertheless remain imaginary, as the title tells us. Indeed, the wish to write a poem that represents the unrepresentative self-sufficiency of poetry must inevitably melt into self-ironizing paradox, as Bishop seems finally to sense in the poem's closing lines:

> Icebergs behoove the soul
> (both being self-made from elements least visible)
> to see them so: fleshed, fair, erected indivisible.

Icebergs, apparently the unimaginary kind, may behoove us to *see* both them and the art they can represent as self-begotten, but for us to see them as self-begotten is not for them to be that way. We may have to imagine the six-sevenths of an iceberg that doesn't show above the sea, but by most people's philosophy that doesn't make it any less there, or at least any less capable of sinking our ship, of showing fatally what Dr. Johnson learned more easily by striking his foot against what he called a disproof of Bishop Berkeley.[1] Still, Bishop the poet feels too committed to her fantasy to end in any merely easy lament that it fails, for she paradoxically juxtaposes her lament with a retracting parenthesis that itself gives a further paradox. Her assertion that the soul and the icebergs are self-made contradicts the implication that we only *see* them that way, and yet in itself that assertion rests upon a prior or interior contradiction, the impossible conjunction of "self-made" with self-made "from."

Making of any kind, let alone self-making, is a problem, Bishop knows, for she senses its root paradox—that whenever we *make*, we make *from*, and yet if we make from, then in some sense we never truly make, never create. In no poem does that paralyzing insight more unnerve her than in "The Weed," one of her most haunting poems, and one that cries out the anguish before creation that characterizes so much modern poetry. But "The Weed" has not been much discussed or anthologized, perhaps because it strays so far from the image of Bishop as "femininely" poised and placid.

"The Weed" begins with an odd mixture of dreamy vagueness and cold certainty:

> I dreamed that dead, and meditating,
> I lay upon a grave, or bed,

    (at least, some cold and close-built bower).
    In the cold heart, its final thought
    stood frozen, drawn immense and clear,
    stiff and idle as I was there;
    and we remained unchanged together
    for a year, a minute, an hour.

Bishop shocks us (no gentleness here) right from the beginning by bluntly and even casually claiming to recall a dream of a future so extreme—death—that it would leave her no recollection to recall, by taking us to a realm we can so little conceive that we might consider it void of the consciousness that affords imagination any meaning in the first place. All this makes the more surprising her reference, in passing, to unstartled and even ordinary consciousness—"and meditating." As an opening this recalls Dickinson's archly offhand " 'Twas just this time last year I died."[2] For such boldness, Bishop's claim of mere dream seems apologetic and trivializing. It helps us accommodate or naturalize the initial shock in a way that reassures but also disappoints, recalling the inexperienced writer's familiar announcement at the end that everything we had found interesting was only a dream and so could be explained away. But when Bishop *begins* by confessing to such apology, she alerts us that dream here might mystify as much as it explains, that it takes us to and not from what troubles.

    In particular, dream here mystifies where she is: "a grave, or bed." Grave seems natural enough, at least for someone dead, but "or bed" shocks because, while it makes a natural enough link to dream or dying and so fits the defensively ordinary side of dreamy association, it makes a horrible link to grave, tying the place of love to the place not of dying but of endless death, a chilling conjunction like that the husband of Frost's aptly titled "Home Burial" makes between graveyard and bedroom as he speaks to his estranged wife. The word "bed" strikes the more strongly for coming after the more expectable "grave," which might tame bed if it came after it, and by rhyming internally—as Bishop often does—with the word it so jars against, "dead." The real subject, in other words, quickly changes from death to love and to the death of love, suggesting not just the end of love but also, and more frighteningly, an actual deathliness in love.

    For Bishop clings to oddly defensive generalities. She says not "in my" grave but "upon a" grave, and not "my" heart but "the" heart, as if something more lies at stake here than how she herself feels or than how she feels at that moment, after, say, an especially rough day. This is forever. Even "a minute, an hour, a year," by its quotidian progression, would suggest simply a long time, but Bishop's reversal to "a year, a minute, an hour," as more subtly in "a grave, or bed," refreshes what had been inconceivable, refreshes what it means for time to remain unchanged forever[3] in the same way Dickinson, from another grave, placidly announces the eternal at the end of "Because I could not stop for Death" (poem 712):

> We paused before a house that seemed
> A swelling of the ground;
> The roof was scarcely visible,
> The cornice but a mound.
>
> Since then 'tis Centuries; but each
> Feels shorter than the day
> I first surmised the horses' heads
> Were toward eternity.

Dickinson, or her voice, rests innocent of any recognition of grave or death. She lands us in forever with appalling gentleness, like one accustomed to the thought, by postponing the awful word to the last and leaving it somehow suspended and unsatisfactory, with its odd off-rhyme with "Day" (and—in Johnson's more accurate edition, which Bishop hadn't yet seen—with an inconclusive but absolute final dash where early editors placed a period). Bishop begins in similar suspension, but not quite so eerily relaxed, for she sustains much uncertainty amidst the certainty of forever. Where Dickinson hints that eternity feels so brief it hardly matters, and her calm, paradoxically, carries a tragic sense of deprivation, Bishop hints nothing of brevity. Her heart's last thought—whatever arbitrary thing it might have been, a fly's buzz or a lover's lament   sticks weightily "unchanged," "immense" and coldly "final," dark where Dickinson's is almost sunny. Even after all that time (or perhaps because Bishop's words are rather a *dream* of all that time), she doesn't know for sure where she is, whether in the first place and moment of immortal forever—a grave, or in the potentially last place and moment of mortal temporality—a bed. She knows instead a mere, even parenthetical minimum "(at least, some cold and close-built bower)," which reinforces the till then uncertainly sexual hint of bed, but in a frightened way, for it combines unemotional cold with the conventionally poetic bed of hot pastoral sexuality. She extends that antithesis as she moves to her heart, emblem of warmth, life, and love, and calls it cold and frozen, merely "the."

Indeed, cold though that heart is, she refers to it as though it were another person who keeps her company. She describes it as curiously animated, with an independent will like the heart in George Herbert's "Love-unknowne," her acknowledged model. But while we all expect to die into some state beyond thought, we wouldn't normally expect her death beyond thought to share its realm with some other part of her that could still think, even if it thinks idly and stiffly; nor would we expect an *it* to think at all. Love here is too dead— whether she lies in bed and is dead only metaphorically, or lies in a grave—for her word "we" to carry any suggestion of company. For if "we" means her and some other thing she calls her heart, then her pluralizing of what people usually consider aspects of a singular self strangely separates her self from her emotions. Still, to the extent "we" means what it usually means, her and some other person, then the link between bed and her frozen heart grows all the more telling, and the whole dream shows more clearly as a metaphor of the death of love in life. It bemoans the death of love in general and, implicitly, the threatening, potentially general death of a particular love. Both senses of "we" ring through these lines, and both strip or defensively try to strip the self of feeling, so defensively that they even foist the lack onto a heart projected and separately animated outside the self.

The self, then, resigns (or pretends or tries to resign) will. It discovers itself as something other than that part of self that does the discovering, much as Dickinson's voice in "I died for beauty, but was scarce" (poem 449), soon after death, discovers a curiously separate and parallel companion who says he died for truth, a kinsman with whom she must remain "unchanged together" for eternity. Dickinson's two voices (echoing the final lines from Keats's "Ode on a Grecian Urn") have nothing and everything to do with each other, and so do Bishop's. Every insistence or defensively casual hint Bishop makes that her heart is not her self underlines the painful feeling that really her heart is her self, and yet that it has an animated will independent of some other and here articulate self. Every "a" and "the" and "its" where we would expect "my" only makes us more aware that "my" is what she means and cannot bear to think. The general, aimed to evade the particular, instead only disguises it until its odd costume makes us notice it the more. It is an old and sometimes frightening argument: I didn't do it, something else forced me, I was possessed.

If something happens, therefore, she not only acts or feels surprised, but she also feels herself as object rather than subject of her own acts:

> Suddenly there was a motion,
> as startling, there, to every sense
> as an explosion. Then it dropped
> to insistent, cautious creeping
> in the region of the heart,
> prodding me from desperate sleep.
> I raised my head. A slight young weed
> had pushed up through the heart and its
> green head was nodding on the breast.
> (All this was in the dark.)
> It grew an inch like a blade of grass;
> next, one leaf shot out of its side
> a twisting, waving flag, and then
> two leaves moved like a semaphore.
> The stem grew thick. The nervous roots
> reached to its side; the graceful head
> changed its position mysteriously,
> since there was neither sun nor moon
> to catch its young attention.
> The rooted heart began to change
> (not beat) and then it split apart
> and from it broke a flood of water.

The power of the weed rises from within her, from within her body and within her self. Yet she acts not only innocent of it but even afraid of it. She fears, then, not some alien plant. Rather, she fears herself, her own power and imagination, her own body. Or one part of herself fears some other part, for her own power tears her, literally splits her in two, into herself and her so-called "heart," or into herself and, as she calls it, "the heart" in "the breast." Some threateningly invasive and independent part of her assumes all the power that the rest of her might wish for, but with a daemonic force, a force of possession, a power creative in that it grows wondrously, and yet one that destroys and usurps her self by an agency that nevertheless is born of what it destroys. What kind of power can do all that? What terrifies Bishop in this nightmare? What is this weed?

It must be many things. It is, indeed, a weed. And it seems also to be her own creativity, her imagination run amok and her body, she fears, run amok too. It seems, in other words, to be her poetic power, and also pregnancy.

A fetus—if there were one (and whether there was doesn't matter here, for she would suspect that there *could* be)—would feel like part of her and yet would also feel bizarrely independent, with its own animated will. It would grow, emotionally, from her heart's will, divide her in two, invade what had been hers alone and—if she didn't want it or wasn't sure—it would possess her like some gentler version of the exorcist's daemon, be born of her and yet in its creative power seem to usurp her. Our critical tradition takes the poem as the ultimate act of creation, perhaps partly because men have defined that tradition, but a woman anxious about love has a more corporeal stake in her anxiety over creativity than a man does.[4]

Yet this is, of course, a literary as well as a corporeal matter. In a poem, a woman anxious about creativity, bodily or otherwise, is anxious about poetry, and from the beginning of her career, in such poems as "The Map" and "The Imaginary Iceberg," Bishop felt preoccupied with the status of poetry, with wondering assertions of its adequacy and sufficiency that, as we have seen, expose her doubt as much as her confidence. She knows not whether she be the Man-Moth, or the Man ("The Man-Moth"). Any man or woman might fear to scale a building, but no moth need fear it. If a moth falls, it can rise to fly again, but when a man—or woman—falls, she will land where, unlike in "The Weed," death will be no dream.

Thus from early in her career Bishop feels extraordinarily anxious about the place and power of poetry and whether she can gain access to—and survive—that power. She frequently complained about her meager production, writing Marianne Moore that "it's as if all the nouns were there but the verbs were lacking."[5] She even left an unpublished poem, fittingly unfinished, in which, languishing in Brazil, she complains that she can't finish a poem and pleads for

help from her two closest poet friends back in the states, Moore and
the prolific Robert (Cal) Lowell:

> and I am sick of myself,
> and sometime during the night
> the poem I was trying to write
> has turned into prepositions:
> ins and aboves and upons
>
> what am I trying to do?
> Change places in a canoe?
>   method of composition —
>
>   .   .   .   .
>
> Marianne, loan me a noun!
> Cal, please cable a verb!
> Or simply propulse through the ether
> some more powerful meter
>
> The radio battery is dead . . . [6]

Moore is the poet of detailed observation — nouns, and Lowell the
poet of bold assertion — verbs and drum-beat meter. It seems to
Bishop, for this moment at least, that they write the poems, while
she worries over petty things like prepositions. Her battery feels
dead, her ambition unfulfillable. Cynically, she accuses herself of a
mere jittery carefulness more appropriate to changing places in a
canoe than to real poetic grandeur. She feels the pull of ambition,
but something keeps her from following it.

"The Man-Moth," much more deeply concerned with the fear of
ambition, startles us with its brilliant and brilliantly evoked invention,
its more tender reincarnation of Kafka's *The Metamorphosis*. Yet
Bishop, like her own invented hybrid, nervously scales the ominous
implications of her poem. She turns curiously sentimental at the end
and — in this poem that blames us for our fear of ambition — passes
off or apologizes for her imagination in a footnote that names her
source as a newspaper misprint for "mammoth." No doubt she enjoys
the printer's slip as one of those comical foibles of ordinary life. And
yet, the curious modesty in her wish to credit circumstance with the
impetus for her own imagination suggests that she also wants to say
she wouldn't really think up anything so strange herself and can't
be blamed for it, and after all there really is no such thing, it's only

a mistake. The waking world, she implies, will not permit such dreams. In "Sleeping Standing Up," she says that "As we lie down to sleep the world turns half away," releasing "dreams, contrived to let us do / so many a dangerous thing"—dangerous things, implicitly, that we dare not do while awake, and that in "The Weed" she loses all power *not* to do.

The figure of the weed curiously inverts and mocks the Romantic trope of organic poetic imagination and joins it to the allegorical mode of daemonic possession,[7] thus mocking the received Romantic confidence—or at least the Romantic pretense of confidence—in the efficacy and availability of poetic imagination and of poetry itself.

M. H. Abrams, in *The Mirror and the Lamp*, traces the growth of organic metaphors for poetic imagination, images of animals and more often of plants, describing how such images sprout in Edward Young's *Conjectures on Original Composition* (1759) and gradually replace more mechanical metaphors until they flower forth in Coleridge's critical prose as the dominant Romantic trope for poetic invention.[8] Abrams thus gives an invaluable history of the figure Bishop appropriates in "The Weed." To understand her poem and how it comments on poetic tradition, it will help to look at Abrams's account closely. Bishop, indeed, read Coleridge energetically and cited Herbert as a model for "The Weed" by way of citing Coleridge's discussion of Herbert.[9]

Abrams might appear to write objective history, but his story, as he tells it, tacitly takes Coleridge as its hero and organicism as its cause. For although he shows the failings of metaphors for mechanical imagination, the failings that prompt Coleridge and others to invoke organic metaphors instead, Abrams hardly more than glances at any difficulties with the idea of invention as organic. As a result, his story carries an implicit, ideal teleology, in which truth is the goal and Coleridge takes us to it. Once we have reached it, in Coleridge, the story pretty much closes, as if that were the end of Abrams's account not because he only happens to be talking about metaphors of invention through the Romantics in general and Coleridge in particular, but rather because Coleridge takes us to the end of what we can wisely think on the subject. Abrams's method is historical in the old sense, with little address to historiographical principles. He chronicles the development or progression or growth of ideas, proceeding as if by his advantage of knowledge alone, independent of any impulse from method. Rather neatly, then, such a historiography itself participates in the organicism it describes. A reader might well ask whether Abrams's method is the consequence, the aptly neutral unveiler, of the history he presents with apparent objectivity, or whether it precedes and thus partly and subjectively creates that history. Is his exposition of the mirror and the lamp—and exaltation of the lamp—itself a mirror, as his stance ironically implies, or has his own work become another lamp?[10]

For Abrams's history, to which we remain much in debt, sometimes seems curiously neat. Organic art, as he reports it, sounds rather happy and untroubled.[11] He notes, though, that Coleridge was at some pains to insist that organic metaphors of imagination describe the imagining mind as subject to the will, as willfully judging how to relate the parts to each other and to the whole, and not as passively receiving a natural outgrowth of some fated blueprint from the seed.[12]

Much is at stake here, and much in particular that Bishop dramatizes in "The Weed." One of Coleridge's most eloquent pleas for the organicism of imagination comes in his lecture "Shakespeare's Judgment Equal to His Genius," where the pains stand out more than the pleading. In that lecture, Coleridge is adamantly on the defensive. He sounds afraid, and we might ask why. To be sure, he has a point about Shakespeare, a well-taken point that much needed to be made: he defends Shakespeare's art against the common and silly idea that Shakespeare is a mere and accidental natural. But Coleridge surely has a stake in his argument, just as others have a stake in seeing Shakespeare as a natural genius. If Shakespeare is a natural genius, then we can excuse ourselves for not being Shakespeares. If Shakespeare is a deliberate artist, then art is subject to will and Coleridge can see himself as happily in control of his own by then dwindling art. But, of course, the onetime poet of "Kubla Khan" knows better, knows how the best of his imagination depends on some part of it he cannot understand, and wishes fearfully that he could control and recover the powers he has lost. He even has an organic metaphor for such a threateningly natural and uncontrollable imagination, one that he uses (in words Abrams does not quote) to oppose his claim for controlled imagination (that Abrams does quote). He calls it a weed.[13]

Coleridge's defensiveness thus points to a latent fright in the

Romantics' organic metaphors of imagination that Abrams underestimates and that Bishop's poem digs out. Even Edward Young,
Abrams's harbinger for Coleridge, writes his *Conjectures on Original
Composition* hardly at all to promote the metaphor that Abrams
astutely observes. He too writes in fear, and much more forthrightly
than Coleridge, because Young's dominant theme is that writers of
the present age need not be inhibited by writers of the past—which
is to observe, of course, that they are inhibited. The metaphor of
imagination as organic, other writers sensed, could even suggest a
threat, a loss of control.[14] Hence a somewhat later Romantic, Hawthorne, has his doubly belated (imaginatively and erotically) villain,
a parody of Wordsworth who dismally chooses to be called Chillingworth, speak in terms that show what Bishop senses and Coleridge
tries to deny about organic metaphors of imagination. Asked where
he found some herbs, the nature-haunting Chillingworth answers:
" 'Here at hand. . . . I found them growing on a grave, which bore
no tombstone, nor other memorial of the dead man, save these ugly
weeds that have taken upon themselves to keep him in remembrance.
They grew out of his heart, and typify, it may be, some hideous
secret that was buried with him, and which he had done better to
confess during his lifetime.' "[15] Hawthorne, as the author of such
stories as "Egotism, or the Bosom Serpent" and "Rappaccini's Daughter," with its suggestions of cross-species incest between Rappaccini's
plants and Rappaccini's daughter, knew how to think of the self as
violated and invaded, and even as violated and invaded by some
serpent of itself.

Like Hawthorne's, then, Bishop's weed uproots the other side of
Coleridge's happy metaphor, showing it as not so inevitably happy,
and as not necessarily even organic in the full sense that Coleridge
and Abrams imply. For Coleridge and Abrams see the organicism
of art in a way that much recent criticism has grown skeptical (or
sometimes even scornful) of, as suggesting an organic *unity*.[16] But
as soon as our vegetable metaphor becomes a *weed* instead of some
vague plant or tree, it releases a sense of violation and usurpation.
Moreover, though Abrams and Coleridge, as well as Keats, Shelley,
and others, most frequently use plants for their organic metaphors
of creativity, when Bishop grafts any plant, let alone a weed, to her
own animal body, she fleshes out the full range of the organic met-

aphor's suggestiveness by setting together so uneasily two breeds of the organic that can never be spliced into a unity.

Something fills her body that threatens to become a part, even a source of that body, and yet that feels independent of her body as she customarily thinks of it, something like a fetus, and like another thing yet more anterior, the other source of a fetus: a phallus. "The stem grew thick. The nervous roots / reached to each side; the graceful head / changed its position mysteriously." Such mysterious moving suggests the way a phallus can seem independent of a man's body, let alone independent of the woman's body it might nevertheless enter. Either way, fetus or phallus, she—the whole of her, body and mind—feels a loss in the singularity, the organicism, of self. She is out of control in a way that coitus and pregnancy or the act of creation itself might well figure—creation of any kind, bodily or poetic.

Accordingly, creativity can release a buried part of self that belittles the ordinary will we tend to identify with self. As Bishop wrote, using a weedlike metaphor in an undergraduate essay not long before writing "The Weed," "The crises of our lives . . . crop up unexpected and out of turn, and somehow or other arrange themselves according to a calendar we cannot control."[17] The fear of pregnancy, natural to some degree for any woman, feels especially powerful for women who don't want their calendars so invaded or changed. Together with the fear of (and fascination with) sexuality so common in American writing, in a poem the fear of pregnancy can suggest an anxiety as well over literary creativity. Bishop is by no means the first to make such a connection or feel such a threat. Mary Shelley, perhaps, made it the most memorably.

When she conceived *Frankenstein* at age eighteen, Mary Shelley had been with Percy Shelley for two years, spent most of that time pregnant, and no doubt could foresee that she would spend most of her near future pregnant as well.[18] She wrote the story of a man who conceives a monster—the common term until recently for a horribly deformed baby—and who describes himself as feeling the "never-dying worm alive in my bosom," and says he "bore a hell within me, which nothing could extinguish" because of the "fiend that lurked in my heart." All this, he claims at the end, is the spawn of his ambition, and so he cautions the man who tells his tale to "avoid ambition"; and then, after he dies, the cast-off monster of his ambition comes forth to say that "I, the miserable and the abandoned, am an abortion."[19] Mary Shelley had plenty of profoundly ordinary reasons to fear pregnancy, but as the daughter of two famous writers (Mary Wollstonecraft and William Godwin) and the unauthorized companion (later wife) of another, she also had extraordinary imaginative reasons to fear it, given the association between bodily and literary creativity.

Her introduction, written some fifteen years later, shows how deeply, and by then, at least, unconsciously, she made that association. She recalls how she and Percy and their friend Byron all challenged each other to write a ghost story, but she couldn't think of one. There could hardly be any more striking instance of an emerging writer's anxiousness about her own imaginative power. The challenge forces the occasion; she cannot wait. And she cannot wait because the abstract competition that all writers, let alone beginning writers, feel with their peers and forebears is for her absolutely literalized. So much so that even our current idea that such competition becomes a literary version of Freud's sexually charged family contest doubles over, for Mary Shelley, on her unliterary sexuality. She competes not just with any forebears and potential peers, but instead with her own lover and his friend Byron, the vaunted roué who had just begot a child on her own stepsister. It is no wonder, then, that Mary Shelley felt not just her ability to write a ghost story at stake but even her ability to write at all. And so, as she recalls her troubles with the ghost story, she expands to a meditation on the impossibility of any true creativity:

> I thought and pondered—vainly. I felt that blank incapability of invention which is the greatest misery of authorship, when dull Nothing replies to our anxious invocations. *Have you thought of a story?* I was asked each morning, and each morning I was forced to reply with a mortifying negative.
>
> Everything must have a beginning, . . . and that beginning must be linked to something that went before. . . . Invention, it must be humbly admitted, does not consist in creating out of void, but out of chaos; the materials must, in the first place, be afforded: it can give form to dark, shapeless substances, but cannot bring into being the substance itself.

If she cannot think of a story, she uses her failure, defensively, as a chance to observe that no one ever really thinks of a story.

But that very struggle gives rise to the plot of her novel, in a connection that follows directly in her introduction but that she doesn't make herself. For she next describes how she went to bed — a tangibly thought-of bed, for though she doesn't mention (and probably couldn't, for decorum) sharing it with Percy, she still says that "When I placed my head on my pillow I did not sleep." Lying then in bed, probably beside the father of her children, who is also her competition and complement in love and imagination, she imagines a "student" (as in some sense she is to Percy and Byron) who creates from the parts of corpses the "hideous phantasm of a man."

> His success would terrify the artist; he would rush away from his odious handiwork, horror-stricken. He would hope that, left to itself, the slight spark of life which he had communicated would fade, that this thing which had received such imperfect animation would subside into dead matter, and he might sleep in the belief that the silence of the grave would quench forever the transient existence of the hideous corpse which he had looked upon as the cradle of life. He sleeps; but he is awakened; he opens his eyes; behold, the horrid thing stands at his bedside, opening his curtains and looking on him with yellow, watery, but speculative eyes. I opened mine in terror.[20]

She opens her eyes to escape the vision, but that act so closely repeats the act in her waking dream that she herself becomes the mad creator (whom she would later dub Frankenstein). They both open their eyes from bed to monster, from the place of sex to its feared consequence: the production of a hideous progeny that itself then becomes — since it gives her a subject for her ghost story and novel — her literary progeny. Such literary progeny should then relieve the fear that she cannot create, but the toil of creation turns out not to be so pure. Creation, the "cradle of life," has brought her too much pain. So that instead of showing up a smiling, cuddly baby, it shows up an odious handiwork, a hideous animation, a monster, or, from Bishop's later bed, a weed.

The birthing of babies and poems does not altogether yield happiness, Mary Shelley and Elizabeth Bishop imply. Perhaps they see that more easily than their male counterparts do, at least when considering the analogy between bodily and poetic birthing. A few

years after *Frankenstein,* Percy Shelley, in "A Defense of Poetry,"
equated poetry with pleasure, and then said that the "poetical fac-
ulty" "grows under the power of the artist as a child in the mother's
womb, and the very mind which directs the hands in formation is
incapable of accounting to itself for the origin, the gradations, or
the media of the process."[21] Like Abrams and Coleridge,[22] then,
Percy Shelley implies that unconscious imagination works rather
happily, but Mary Shelley's and Bishop's anxious recastings suggest
that that is not always the case.

"Suddenly," says Bishop, "there was a motion, / as startling, there,
to every sense / as an explosion." *She* explodes, but she says "there
was," not "I did," for though the exploding thing is a part of her,
until this moment of upheaval it remains an unconscious part, and
so genuinely unconscious that she can hardly acknowledge it as hers
at all. She says "to *every* sense," raises her head to *look,* and recognizes
what she claims to see as a weed, describing its motions in detail
and calling it green, "all this" though she also says she lies in the
dark, where presumably she cannot see. Hence the weed she describes
as apart from her cannot be only some surreal other but must be
also an eruption of projected self, as later she more or less admits:
"I could see / (or, in that black place, thought I saw)." Her erupted
self signals a fundamental change in her world. Everything starts
doubling. First the weed splits her, and then the weed's "one leaf,"
a "waving flag," splits into "two leaves" that move "like a semaphore," suggesting not an opaque obscurity but rather an interpretable code. And then the ominously "rooted heart"—a phrase
that implies a strangling into emotional stagnation—the heart that
already sprouts the splitting weed and splitting woman, itself breaks,
and into a flood that in turn will branch into two rivers. Thus the
narrating consciousness darkly envisions herself almost as a serially
bifurcating equivalent of the impossible Man-Moth: a plant-person,
a weed-woman, condemned to some bizarre kind of infinite cross-
phylum mitosis that explodes upon what she had taken for infinite
stagnation. And that explosion, she says, wakes her from her "desperate sleep."

Her waking drastically intensifies the conflict, for if the dream
ends and the horrors do not, then she must give up any remnant of
hope that those horrors are *only* a dream. No wonder her sleep was

desperate; she feared to wake. Once she opens her eyes, she trembles to discover whether the nightmarish riot will continue. And so her tone marks that half-aware sense of discovery we often feel in waking, especially in a strange place, as she raises her head to see her newfound world, and turns from language of disruption, from words like *suddenly, startling,* and *explosion,* to a different language. For the first time, she uses a short sentence: "I raised my head." Its brevity sticks out by the way it begins at the start of a line and stops sharply in the middle; and its small, wary action evokes how she does not yet know or dare predict what she'll see. She continues that tentativeness with an uncertain language of modest discovery: words like *slight, young,* and the guarded, parenthetical cautioning that "(All this was in the dark)." Understatedly, she extends the tentativeness still more through the way *dark* chimes gently by an assonance with *heart* that suggests but doesn't quite give a standard end-rhyme.

But she finds herself in a world at least as strange as the one she had supposedly been dreaming, so that her waking might be just another part of her dream. Or perhaps she was never dreaming in the first place. Or the waking and dreaming worlds are equally askew. Whichever, her suspension among such possibilities can hardly matter; for they all amount to the same miserable grotesque. Her waking had seemed to promise a fundamental change, but the only change it brings is the discovery that no change can relieve her pain and bewilderment. Thus to the poem's narrating mind the unconscious powers of imagination yield no pleasure. To Bishop, though, we can assume that the apparently painful imagining still yields a great deal of pleasure. For she still chooses the work of writing the poem and chooses to publish it. Even if the poem in itself only hurts her (which seems unlikely), the completion and publishing of it bring her pleasure.[23]

And so the unconscious resources of imagination offer Bishop a complicated mix of rewards and pains, all figured in the startling arousal of an interior self—something we usually seek to uncover, and in a growing plant—something poets have long romanticized. But for Bishop that inner plant shoots up into a hideous weed she hasn't sought at all. Bishop's eery metaphor of vegetable and corporeal self-celebration and self-chastisement revises the standard pattern of such imagery, as we have seen, but she still has a powerful precursor in Whitman, especially in a poem like "Scented Herbage of My Breast" (1860).

Vegetation figures throughout *Leaves of Grass;* Bishop's words in "The Weed," though common words enough, cannot help recalling Whitman's very title: ". . . like a blade of grass; / next, one leaf shot out. . . ." To be sure, Whitman often uses plants as innocent metaphors of his supposedly undaunted imagination, especially in his preface to the first edition of *Leaves of Grass* in 1855. But over the next decade Whitman's confidence in his poetic power erodes, and the troubles stand out in his poems less intermittently, less surreptitiously:

> Scented herbage of my breast,
> Leaves from you I glean, I write, to be perused best afterwards,
> Tomb-leaves, body-leaves growing up above me above death,
> Perennial roots, tall leaves, O the winter shall not freeze you delicate
>   leaves,
> Every year shall you bloom again . . .
> O slender leaves! O blossoms of my blood! I permit you to tell in your
>   own way of the heart that is under you,
> O I do not know what you mean there underneath yourselves, you
>   are not happiness,
> You are often more bitter than I can bear, you burn and sting me
>   . . .[24]

Whitman, like Bishop, claims to lie both dead and conscious. His leaves sprout from his lifeless breast and flower almost explicitly into the metaphor that Bishop represses—into the leaves of grass that are his imagination, his poems, as the title of his book tells us—and into the metaphor of book leaves or pages that his title grows from. Like Bishop's weed, but again more explicitly, Whitman's leaves tell no happy tale, but instead speak his heart's bitterness. Thus Whitman looms large behind Bishop in his insistence on literalizing the linked metaphorical chain of body, plant, and poem. Like Bishop, he feels an abject loss of will. As the poem concludes, he faces even that more squarely than she does, addressing death in deep resignation to it. And he connects death to love: "Give me your tone therefore O death, that I may accord with it, / Give me yourself, for I see that you belong to me now above all, and are folded inseparably together, you love and death are . . ." (lines 28-29). Whitman's likeness to Bishop underscores that the pairing of breast and heart with death, in both poems, speaks grimly about the fate of those emotions we connect with the heart. For all Bishop's surrealist drama, Whitman's franker and more melancholy way brings out the sadness of her poem.

In her sadness, her tone remains oddly flat, with an unsettling disparity between the threatening events she describes and the air of distanced reason she describes them in. She carefully works through logical distinctions ("was made / itself") and parenthetical qualifications; and she is quick to mute the interruption from "Suddenly . . . an explosion" with a retraction in "Then it dropped." Amidst the strange threats she describes, such caution encodes its calm as a mask for agony.

As she realizes that even though she wakes, nothing fundamental has altered, that her dead heart can change but never again can beat, then her heart breaks. That is the proverbially coded fate of hearts,[25] perhaps the interpretable code signified by the leafy semaphore, and it returns her poem, as Whitman turns his, to the lament for a love, or for love in general. It breaks not into a flower, which would continue—and tame—the botanic metaphor, but into a flood, as in a violent birth. The image so changes, or seems to change, that in the rush of water "The weed was almost swept away." But that makes yet another continuity in the guise of change, for as the woman spawns a weed that threatens to destroy her, so the weed itself is subject to the same destruction by its own erupting pregnancy that so surprises and uproots the woman. Such latent powers, whether or not we think of them as modes of pregnancy, image forth the continuing weight of the past on the present. If nothing changes, then we can only repeat.

"The Weed" thus recounts the discovery of the past in what was mistaken for an independent present. The water brings a new vision, but like everything else, it turns out to be only a newly known vision of the old:

> A few drops fell upon my face
> and in my eyes, so I could see
> (or in that black place, thought I saw)

that each drop contained a light,
a small, illuminated scene;
the weed-deflected stream was made
itself of racing images.
(As if a river should carry all
the scenes that it had once reflected
shut in its waters, and not floating
on momentary surfaces.)

We are caught in a chain of images. The weed had seemed *merely*
an image, a metaphor, so that what breaks out in opposition to it
might look more concrete, more absolute; but it too is made of images.
Every "scene" is a "seen"—a projection into the dark—and not
somehow inherent whether seen or not. Perhaps there can therefore
be no true change; something so vaguely there in the first place
cannot disappear. There can be only accumulation. We can have
more of things, but we cannot switch entirely to different things.
The past cannot be erased, it cannot fade, can never be evaded or
truly forgotten, and if repressed, then, as Freud said, in some way
it will return, as it returns to make the subject of this poem. Bishop
feels here—and imagines feeling even after death—the oppression
or irrevocability of the past. Here she explicitly is not the poet of
mere surface images that she so often sounds like in our usual
responses to her. The past rules her. She cannot rule herself, which
might help explain why she so often, in other poems, resorts to the
poetry of surface images that she here implies is defensive and
evasive.

Prominent in all our pasts, of course, is our birth—supposedly
our greatest trauma; and we have seen how profoundly uneasy Bishop
feels in "The Weed" about the prospect of bringing a new organic
body through that process, and returning her own to it again, this
time from the other side, giving from her body to another instead
of receiving her body from another. Either way points out some
absolute limit to our corporeal independence, and hence also to our
independence in any terms. The anxieties over creativity and pregnancy implied in "The Weed," together with the related fear of
losing control, figure for Bishop a specially feminine vulnerability,
a maternal and corporeal uneasiness that shows up frequently in her
poems, and yet has little to do with the way her poems have usually

been discussed. Sometimes such issues obviously dominate a poem, as in "In the Waiting Room." Other times she disguises them by the distraction of bizarre events, as in "The Weed," or raises them less directly, as in the third of her "Songs for a Colored Singer." In that song, a World War II lullaby so gentle that, like the baby, we can respond to its restfulness without noticing the anger, a mother (apparently) sings that "The shadow of the crib makes an enormous cage / upon the wall." When the wall looks ominously like an adult-sized extension of the baby's cage, it suggests that the mother lies imprisoned by her home and baby, versus, presumably, the father and his dubious freedom to go off to war. Similarly, in the fourth song, she rewrites "The Weed" as a lyric, softening its explosiveness:

> What's that shining in the leaves,
> the shadowy leaves,
> like tears when somebody grieves,
> shining, shining in the leaves?
>
>   .   .   .   .
>
> See it lying there like seeds,
> like black seeds.
> See it taking root like weeds.
>
>   .   .   .   .
>
> Fruit or flower? It is a face.
> Yes, a face.
> In that dark and dreary place
> each seed grows into a face.

Here she repeats the weed, the oddly independent growing, the dark, the uncertainty, and the transformation into something seemingly fetal and human. Someone might conclude, however, that these poems, though among Bishop's best, are far from representative, that more often her poems are understated, almost actionless.

For now, it will serve to take one much-admired poem that typifies Bishop's quieter work, and view it through the perspective applied to and developed from "The Weed." Let us look at "Filling Station." It is remarkably consonant with what we have been discussing in "The Weed," and such a consistency across Bishop's oeuvre can encourage us to revise how her work is usually seen. I am trying, frankly, to do for Bishop something akin to what Lionel Trilling did for Robert Frost.[26] People had long read Frost too exclusively as a

pleasant and pretty poet, a coffee-table book lover of nature, and
then Trilling showed that Frost is terrified, and terrified of nature
especially. Bishop, as I have been suggesting, is terrified too, and
much like Frost, as we shall see. But the nature she is terrified of,
even in this playful and happy poem—I've tried to choose a seemingly unlikely poem for my point—is potentially her own.

A filling station is a place where you get filled, whether with
gasoline, or with pregnancy of body, or, as in "The Weed," with also
a pregnancy of mind. Going to the filling station provides Bishop
with her occasion for a poem; it gives her a subject, just what in
"The Weed" she seems uncertain she can find enough of. Having
set her scene by the title (though it hasn't yet gathered its resonance),
Bishop begins abruptly in sudden and comically self-mocking
squeamishness and exclamation:

> Oh, but it is dirty!
> —this little filling station,
> oil-soaked, oil-permeated
> to a disturbing, over-all
> black translucency.
> Be careful with that match!
>
> Father wears a dirty,
> oil-soaked monkey suit
> that cuts him under the arms,
> and several quick and saucy
> and greasy sons assist him
> (it's a family filling station),
> all quite thoroughly dirty.
>
> Do they live in the station?
> It has a cement porch
> behind the pumps, and on it
> a set of crushed and grease-
> impregnated wickerwork;
> on the wicker sofa
> a dirty dog, quite comfy.
>
> Some comic books provide
> the only note of color—
> of certain color. They lie

upon a big dim doily
draping a taboret
(part of the set), beside
a big hirsute begonia.

Why the extraneous plant?
Why the taboret?
Why, oh why, the doily?
(Embroidered in daisy stitch
with marguerites, I think,
and heavy with gray crochet.)

Somebody embroidered the doily.
Somebody waters the plant,
or oils it, maybe. Somebody
arranges the rows of cans
so that they softly say:
ESSO—SO—SO—SO
to high-strung automobiles.
Somebody loves us all.

It's a family filling station; right away, dirt and filling and family seem somehow related. Somebody, or some body, has been filled with family, and fills family with something, in a place that otherwise and most of all seems devoted to dirt and oil. That devotion at first makes the station seem wholly a male place, with its father and its saucy and greasy sons (whose grease makes their sauciness a clever pun), but then Bishop notices other signs. The domestic aura of wickerwork has nothing of male dirt to it, let alone the aura of impregnated wickerwork. Or does it? Women don't impregnate themselves here, and this feminine wickerwork is impregnated by the pervasive masculine oil, as if to continue the pun at the center and title of *Moby-Dick*, that book about hunting for sperm oil. A filling station, or womb, here gets filled with masculine grease. In other words, just as Bishop learns in the poem to see the filling station as more than a sign of men, so we should not think that the turning to women makes femininity the poem's or the station's definitive focus. The poem *is* about femininity, but it is also about how the masculine and feminine can fit together, and the kinds of pregnancy such a fit leads to, both bodily pregnancy and the more general pregnancy of female creativity.

Much depends on how we take the ending. When I first read it, I laughed out loud at the final line, and felt delighted at what I took for a trivial and charming little appreciation of motherhood. I mention that response because it may be a common one, and surely there is some truth to it. Bishop is a poet of great charm. But as we ponder the ending it gets more and more suggestive. "Somebody loves us all"—unless the poem's evidence, namely a doily, a taboret, a begonia, and some neatly arranged cans of motor oil, doesn't justify such all-inclusiveness, so that the final line becomes ironic. We can read it with a sarcastic accent on somebody, as if to admit wryly that maybe *somebody* is fool enough to love even this oil-soaked father and his greasy sons.

And who, after all, is somebody? Is that so self-evident? She (if we can risk a pronoun) is never named or identified, and remains, at the last, evasively unspecified: *some*body. It makes a big difference, then, that the last two stanzas turn so largely to the unspecified and interrogative. Can *somebody* refer, ironically, to *nobody*, or, in the other direction, if the greasy men of the filling station seem so unlovable, might there be no one or nothing that could love them except that grand Somebody that supposedly loves *any*one, that is, God? And if the somebody is God, is that comforting, because God's love is a great love, or, in a poem by the poet of "The Unbeliever," does that become only a greater irony, if the love of God is no love we expect to know?

Frost provides a model here, in "Design":

> I found a dimpled spider, fat and white,
> On a white heal-all, holding up a moth
> Like a white piece of rigid satin cloth—
> Assorted characters of death and blight
> Mixed ready to begin the morning right,
> Like the ingredients of a witches' broth—
> A snow-drop spider, a flower like a froth,
> And dead wings carried like a paper kite.
>
> What had that flower to do with being white,
> The wayside blue and innocent heal-all?
> What brought the kindred spider to that height,
> Then steered the white moth thither in the night?

What but design of darkness to appall?—
If design govern in a thing so small.

Like Bishop, Frost begins with the conspicuously minor, an extraneous plant and the connections bred by its odd displacement from the routine, bred, if nowhere else, then in the curious observer. The hirsute begonia seems of a piece with the impregnated wickerwork, the doily, the taboret. The white heal-all, when heal-alls should be blue, and suggesting in its very name a power beyond its tiny size, seems of a piece with the white spider and the white moth. So much so that the odd whiteness of the heal-all seems the cause for the whole scene, the reason why the three little white organisms have all come together in apparent design, in apparent consequence of some will. But Frost shapes his own design—surely one of the inevitable subjects of his poem—with strikingly bold restraint. We generally think of designs, such as doilies or embroidery, as pretty, and so we might be tempted to see beauty in this flowery scene from nature. But Frost says nothing of beauty. Instead he talks of death and blight and witches' broth, of darkness to appall. His own broth, then, is remarkable, in Hawthornean fashion, for how much he implies is possible and how little he commits himself to any of that as actual. Instead, he turns to a series of questions and an *if* that expand his scale from the trivial to the cosmic, without ever sacrificing his aggressive insistence on the trivial, for his final words return to it—"in a thing so small." He thus forces us to ask whether all this is a parody of foolish cosmogonizing, of the way supposedly grand thinkers foist ridiculously vast implications on nature's trifles, as if the arbitrary freaks of chance were somehow willful messages aimed for us to interpret like the dream-weed's semaphore. Or, on the other hand, he forces us to ask whether, if there lies so much design in something so little, there might not lie a correspondingly vast destiny in the larger world of our own lives. Frost does not say. He asks. But, as in Blake's more strident "The Tyger," we can hardly help seeing the blight of his questioning.

Bishop, like Frost, does not say; nor does she confront us so forthrightly as Frost does with the fearful—except, again, by irony. For it seems fearful that the center of her celebration remains unseen, an absence that has almost the same effect as Frost's refusal to answer his questions. Frost's reticence makes us ask about God and the universe, and so does Bishop's. But Bishop also makes us ask about women in the universe of men and men in the universe of women. The woman in "Filling Station" is made representative of women, because we never see her individually, and we know her at all only through the stereotypical leavings of her role. Yet we see her strongly, and that certainty in the midst of absence tells how fully we let role define and confine gender, especially for women. The men here are stereotypes as well, but at least Bishop can see them to confirm it. She never sees the woman, and yet understands as much about her as she understands about the men.[27] And that is frightful, for it defines women as hidden mere somebodies who live *behind* men, maybe live pleasantly, but still are secondary and derivative. And when we recognize them not by themselves but instead by deciphering—easily—a code of their stereotypical role, that shows how utterly our world lives by that code and that role. We do not even need to see the person to know what defines her. Once we determine that a mother is the somebody, then, as implicated readers, we assume we can forecast her from what our world imposes on women and on people who recognize women through those impositions. When without ever having seen her we think that the somebody at least partly suggests a mother, then the powerful implication is that we do not need to see her. The role rules, not the woman.

Still, the role is not purely one of derivation and absence, for Bishop also sees this woman as originating and creative. She artfully arranges the motor oil, she crochets and embroiders a doily, she grows a plant, and she grows children. As in "The Weed," then, Bishop anxiously struggles with the urgency of creativity and the impossibility of true originality. In her story of her own mother, "In the Village," which she placed in her third collection of poems in the same section as "Filling Station," she closely associates a taboret and embroidery with her mother. "In the Village" tells of the four-year-old Bishop meeting the mother she had no memory of, only to have the frightening reentry into her life of that unfamiliar but somehow especially close woman come to a quick halt when her mother collapses mentally and so must go away again. Her mother never recovered, and Bishop never saw her again. In the story she never names her mother, never even refers to or identifies her as her mother. Readers must infer the relation; a few might miss it.

Such odd negligence betrays the child's confusion, her ignorance or repression of who this woman is and how and why they are supposed to feel special to each other.[28] Motherhood, then, for Bishop evokes an ambiguous figure of creativity, and her uneasiness about it has to do with a larger uneasiness about her own imagination.

Indeed, Bishop's work is preoccupied with motherhood, sometimes in the most unlikely contexts. She translated a strange Brazilian story called "The Smallest Woman in the World," where a 17¾-inch woman, who already astonishes the world by her tiny size, astonishes it the more by getting pregnant. When she wrote the Time-Life book on Brazil, she began with an extraordinarily peculiar introduction for a book in such a series, telling about a newborn baby kidnapped from its mother in the maternity ward, and rationalized her use of such a story by claiming that it represents the Brazilian national personality. She carried her preoccupation almost anywhere, apparently without consciousness of it, at one point even trying to write what she called an "awful little story about the artificial insemination of cows."[29] The unseen but much pointed to mother of "Filling Station" thus seems part of a private obsession, perhaps unacknowledged, but still urgently felt as central to Bishop's world.

For the final line of "Filling Station" turns to herself, and to us all. The unexpected cropping up of first person plural at the end is part of what so expands the poem's final import, but in a way so gentle we can almost spoil it by pointing it out. She sustains the subtlety of what could have been a bravura pulling in of her readers by mixing it with that mysterious word *somebody*. The charmingly coy vagueness of that climactic reference monopolizes our attention, so that we take the effect of being brought in ourselves with hardly any notice. Which is partly the point, for the poem is about taking things for granted. We take the work of women for granted, and that work, especially when it is the work of art, turns surreptitious in response. It gains something distinctive that way, but loses much as well. It loses, in Bishop, some species of confidence, or else provides a specially feminine outlet for that crisis of confidence that any poet suffers. For no poet knows for sure where the next poem will come from, or whether it will come at all.

The poet wonders: what will prompt me next? Why, ultimately, the next poem? And the poet of our belated age of anthologies, professional critics, and historians of literature seems to wonder over such questions with a special fear, because it can seem more than ever that the poems have already been written. Can there be new poems? Why will we make them in some way new? The anxiousness of such thoughts enters deeply into many poems of our time, but it seems in Bishop to be the thing that prompts the very poems that worry about it. Why can *I* make a new art? she ponders. Is she truly in control of her imagination, or does it sprout of its own power like a weed? What in her, then, whether under her power or not, will produce it? What in her femininity, in her own filling station of body and mind, will shape her art? And she—this artist whose art's why she does not know, even as she proves again that she is an artist by the poem in which she asks her questions—can she ever rest in the knowledge that she is a poet, or must she always prove it over again?

CHAPTER TWO

Wish: *North & South*

The monument's an object, yet those decorations,
carelessly nailed, looking like nothing at all,
give it away as having life, and wishing. . . .
It is the beginning of a painting,
a piece of sculpture, or poem.

—"The Monument"

I am thinking of being able to write like all the
Authors . . . and where do they get their
imagination and the material.

—"The Sea & Its Shore"

In some ways a poet is by definition a believer, but right at the
beginning of both her first book, *North & South* (1946), and her
collected poems, Bishop hovers just short of some chaotic loss of
control. She describes—we might say she celebrates—a map in
which the printer's "emotion too far exceeds its cause," signifying
some gulf between passion and its occasion.[1] She projects a map—
or "*The* Map," as her title calls it—implicitly of what poetry might
be, especially *her* poetry. But she is not sure. "Land lies in water;
it is shadowed green. / Shadows, or are they shallows. . . ." First she
sees—she is famous for her eye—and then she wonders if she is
wrong. She cannot rest certain. Ordinarily, we might view a map
as an image of objective, recordable certainty; mapmakers observe

and record their observations according to common cartographic convention, and the rest of us follow their records faithfully, with unanxious and unself-conscious belief. But Bishop sees the arbitrariness of maps: "Are they assigned, or can the countries pick their colors?" Bishop refuses belief and makes her poetry of her refusal.

Hence the title and struggle of her early allegory, "The Unbeliever," a poem that in many ways represents the best and most characteristic work in *North & South*. It is a difficult struggle to follow, because the central words come in voices of delusion. Specifically, the poem unfolds through four different voices: the poet's overarching voice, the cloud's, the gull's, and the unbeliever's.[2] The poet's voice at first seems to hold back, to take a neutral, reporter's manner, but the three other voices build a dialogue that gradually enlivens the neutral tone and establishes Bishop's distinctive refusal of belief.

After the overarching voice's introduction, the cloud speaks and Bishop comments:

> "I am founded on marble pillars,"
> said a cloud. "I never move.
> See the pillars there in the sea?"
> Secure in introspection
> he peers at the watery pillars of his reflection.

When clouds talk, we may find ourselves ready to take much for granted; but if we take much for granted in this poem — if we believe much — we will miss much. For when the cloud proclaims that he never moves, he is wrong. Indeed, we don't normally think of clouds as male or thinking or talking; we don't at all define them by gender, mind, or expression. More typically, we associate them with fleeting mobility. Our talking cloud, then, cannot be trusted. Why can he float so far astray in mind as to imagine that in body he goes nowhere? Because, metaphorically, his mind is all he sees; he is "Secure in introspection." When he peers down below him, where potentially he could see something other than himself, it so happens that he sees his reflection in the water. He mistakes his reflected appearance for actual marble pillars, partly because a cloud's variegated hue looks like marble, but also because from his perspective his reflection has the same solidity and constancy as marble. For when he moves, it moves with him. Whenever he looks down at the water, he sees himself reflected, so that he never realizes he has moved. Through a changing world, he sees only himself, and imagines himself unchanged.

Beneath the cloud a gull soars with similar assurance and delusion. These are believers. The gull feels no fear, Bishop implies; he imagines that nothing can block the flight of his imagination. Even the verb he uses for himself, *tower,* by its odd construction from a noun, evokes how he thinks in a wrought vision where fluid things appear as final. But the gull asks the unbeliever what he dreams, which curiously differentiates the gull from the cloud, who gives all to introspection. When the cloud asks a question—" 'See the pillars there in the sea?' "—he is merely rhetorical. He anticipates a simple and certain answer, namely, yes, and he imagines no other possibility. But when the gull asks a question, he has no hint of its answer. Though he shows no rift in his exorbitant confidence, he still shows more curiosity than the cloud. Better to act like the gull, Bishop's allegory suggests, than like the complacent cloud.

The cloud moves, and doesn't know it. The gull moves, and celebrates his movement, and yet his confident celebration implicitly betrays a substitute delusion, for it implies that he cannot imagine anything except that he will move always. He takes his motion as one of the inherent principles of nature. Even his own flight he sees not as some act of his will. *He* doesn't fly. His marble wings fly, and *their* flight carries him, so that, as he sees it, he towers through the sky on marble wings almost as passively as the cloud imagines it rests on marble pillars. Such passivity breeds the errors of vanity, for they see as marble what we would see as least like marble—the infirmest features of themselves, a cloud's reflection or a bird's wing. In their innocent self-obsessions, then—innocent because they see no alternatives—the cloud and the gull see nothing beyond their mistaken images of themselves. And they rest content with that limit. They choose no risks, they hold no doubts. They are believers.

"But," says Bishop as she turns back to not "a" cloud or "a" gull but to *the* unbeliever, the unbeliever sees no such delusions; he doesn't even open his eyes. He cannot, then, even see himself, which suggests that he cannot believe in himself. He keeps his "eyes closed tight," as if he wants not to see, or at least wants not to see outside himself. To the cloud and the gull, outside and inside are all one, all self. By contrast, the unbeliever's fear of sight splits his world in two and implies a deliberate imprisoning in some sense of inner self threatened by the outside. Indeed, the outside magically usurps his power over his own body when he lets down his vigilance in sleep. By falling asleep he loses control, or forfeits the illusion he ever had control, for after telling that the unbeliever "sleeps on the top of a mast," Bishop adds that "Asleep he was transported there." To fall, whether by falling asleep or falling from the mast or both, is—as in "The Weed"—to risk losing your will and subjecting your body to some mysterious ulterior force, even if it is a force you try to escape and deny by "falling" asleep in the first place. Like the cloud and the gull, then, that is, like anyone, the unbeliever has much cause for fear, but unlike the cloud and gull he knows it. No wonder he keeps his eyes closed. No wonder he fears a self that cannot withstand the world outside the self.

But to close your eyes is not to escape the self, any more than the gull and cloud escape their selves by self-flattery. The gull and cloud, with their open eyes, deny their transient selves in favor of silly but comforting illusions. Still, they cannot escape the fate of selves; no illusions will save them from death. They merely think they escape. And when we close our eyes and seal ourselves inside, we release some other and chaotic powers of the self, as in "The Weed." Here, those other powers are dream.

Dream grows in sleep, and we sleep, typically, in bed. We have perhaps been so mesmerized by the supposed exotica of Bishop's mappable geography that we hardly note the resonant ordinariness of her inner geography. In Bishop's poetry, the most typical setting is bed, and the most typical activity, after observation itself, is sleep or arousal from sleep. The waking to a new day's world is often the occasion for or release into the observing that Bishop is more famous for.[3] Her terrified unbeliever thus begins to stand for all those Bishop observers—usually speaking in her own voice—who awake to look at the world anew, often to look down on it from a high place as if looking down at a map, and so to rediscover it empirically. They rediscover with the uncertainty, the unbelief, inevitable in someone who relies empirically on ever-renewing sight instead of on trusted faith. Unlike the cloud and gull and like the sleeper on the mast, they are unbelievers, and to be an unbeliever can be to reduce yourself to your own resources, the most powerful of which is often dream.

Dreamers indulge in what they cannot believe, however much they might suspend their disbelief for the duration of dream; and much of dream's allure comes from that teasing coquetry with belief. In this poem, the dreamer represents that imaginer who courts the most precarious tip of imaginative risk, who, metaphorically, "sleeps on the top of a mast." Poetic imagination is thus at stake in the unbeliever's dream: " 'I must not fall. / The spangled sea below wants me to fall. / It is hard as diamonds; it wants to destroy us all.' " This dreamer fantasizes a hostile world—as the cloud and gull fantasize a world subservient to their own power—so that he might not seem any better off than they are. He might even seem worse off, for they glide contentedly while he cowers in fright. But when we recall how Bishop makes fun of the cloud's and the gull's security, then we might suspect that the unbeliever, for all his delusion and fright, gains something that in their assurance they miss out on.

Trembling on his mast, he in effect invokes Ishmael on the Pequod in *Moby-Dick* (Chapter 35). Ishmael rhapsodizes over the dreamy reverie that his view atop the mast inspires, but then he cautions that such sleepy pleasures can prove fatal to any further pleasure, for one dreamy slip on his narrow perch and the dreamer will perish forever. In part Ishmael simply celebrates the languorous view from ahigh, but he also savors the thrill of the precarious, the romanticized *frisson* that we can win, he suggests, only at the greatest risk, and largely because of that risk. In that way he is much like Bishop's unbeliever, who in effect chooses his risk, as the cloud and the gull deny theirs. They believe; and so they release themselves from relying on original imagination. Though the unbeliever is transported to his mast by some ulterior will while he sleeps, he still chooses his subjection to sleep's dreamy susceptibility. He chooses to keep his eyes shut tight, and within his dream some part of him chooses or wishes for his fear of falling and his fantasy of a voracious diamond sea. By not believing, he implicitly chooses his precarious masthead of imaginative risk; at least he chooses it over the cloud's and the gull's certainty. Like Ishmael, then, he seeks the shudder of danger, even the risk of death, in return for the uprooted perspective it gives him, for the way it liberates his imagination by liberating his vision—even with his eyes closed.

Bishop argues we must yearn after the extreme in experience and perspective to vault our imaginations forward, so that, considering this poem (first published in 1938), it hardly seems surprising that she would give her later years so much to travel and to pursuing places that, for someone from Massachusetts and Nova Scotia, must have felt geographically remote. Like Dickinson, she relishes a slant in her vision. Indeed, Dickinson has a poem curiously almost consonant with "The Unbeliever" (a poem not published until 1945, *after* "The Unbeliever"):

A Pit—but Heaven over it—
And Heaven beside, and Heaven abroad,
And yet a Pit—
With Heaven over it.

To stir would be to slip—
To look would be to drop—
To dream—to sap the Prop
That holds my chances up.
Ah! Pit! With Heaven over it!

The depth is all my thought—
I dare not ask my feet—
'Twould start us where we sit
So straight you'd scarce suspect
It was a Pit—with fathoms under it—
Its Circuit just the same.
Seed—summer—tomb—
Whose Doom to whom?[4]

Dickinson totters on the unbeliever's epitome of the precarious, except that, at least in this poem, she gives no hint she likes it that way, only that it *is* that way. In other, better-known poems she courts pleasure in renunciation and anticipation, as opposed to the security of possession or the traffic of public action. But here she skips reasons and causes. She skips the past and concentrates on that momentary cliff's edge of time before the last future. She describes herself as tenuously suspended in a final, eschatological middle from which she dare not move—and yet, who can *not* move? To inch to any side would be to slip and drop, as it would be for Ishmael or for Bishop's unbeliever. Heaven gleams invitingly beside her and over her, but she has no power to loft herself above her slippery perch. She can jump, we might suppose, but that comically meager option only underlines her peril; it might postpone her impending plunge into the gaping pit, but it will not send her to heaven and it *will* send her right back where she was a moment before, and drop her there even more unsteadily. Paralysis, small comfort that it might be, hardly seems possible—though for the moment she can almost hold still, with the almost-held breath of her short quick lines, all ending with the sharp conclusiveness of consonants (usually *t*, and either *p* or *m* in every other case but line two) and mostly with the hurried sound of accented, one-syllable words and rhymes, most of them finishing with a clipped *t* that gives a trapped sense of rush and abruptness, as wherever she turns she bumps back into the same sounds.

She cannot move to the side, she cannot move up, she cannot not move; that leaves only one thing: collapse into the pit below. And any effort to do anything else will lead her only the more precipitously down. Down is hell, for both Dickinson and Bishop. Bunyan, Bishop's source, has Christian tell Simple, Sloth, and Presumption: "You are like them that sleep on the top of a mast, for the Dead Sea is under you."[5] The Dead Sea in Bunyan's allegory means the sea of dead in hell, where lives of presumption, sloth, or simplicity can lead us. It is where we go when we fall, whether in Dickinson's or Bishop's surreal vignettes or in the emotional or artistic conditions they allegorize. And, as Dickinson's poem can help remind us for Bishop's poem, fall we will, and probably soon, especially if we sleep on masts. For Dickinson imagines no solution, nor does she even pause to lament that she has none. She knows she has none; her concern is not to find solutions but rather to seize the thrill of suffering without them.

That especially links her poem to Bishop's. Though Dickinson relies more on resentment and anger than on unbelief, like Bishop she concentrates on the intensity of imagination in an indifferently hostile universe. As Dickinson clutches at fear's excitement in preference to setting out after utilitarian solutions, so Bishop's unbeliever finds more in his tipsy metaphor of unbelief than she suggests anyone can find through belief. In implicitly—albeit rather discreetly— valorizing her unbeliever, she says nothing of the past and puts all the future at peril, which great sacrifice underlines her unbeliever's immense concentration, like Dickinson's, on the absolutely narrowed moment of the present. That present is grim, the last moment before mortality chops off all sense of *any* changing moments, but its very penultimateness is exactly what both Dickinson and Bishop relish. They seek not final objects so much as imaginative thrill, a thrill of mind rather than a thrill of thing.

But that thrill of mind does not come by itself. And so they betray, even celebrate, a need to induce the thrill. They don't automatically reach the quavering of mind they want, so they cultivate a more accessible, intermediate state that can induce the truer thrill. Holding, or caring for, no vision of a final life, they seek instead some sight of suspended life that can make its own finality, free of eschatology. Imagination reigns, for them, as inherently something in process, incomplete. Completeness would mean imagination's end. The gull and cloud feel complete. They won't fall, at least not in any future they foresee, but who wants a riskless life? Hence Bishop chooses or at least likes unbelief, because it primes her vision. The implications of her choice bear both on Bishop's idea of imagination in general, as something tenuous and unboundable, and on her idea of her own imagination, as something also tenuous, something not sprouting up of its own will, like a weed, but *needing* to be primed, like the breast within which the weed of her poem erupts. She likes the risk of unbelief partly because she does not easily believe in herself, and yet by owning up to that self-doubt, she catapults her powers into something she can believe in; she writes the poem.

The same flight of imaginative anxiety stirs "The Man-Moth," both the poem and its title creature. The Man-Moth, too, lives a life of futile ascent and delusion, and less ambiguously wins Bishop's romanticizing approval for it. That makes his poem easier to read than the unbeliever's, for Bishop keeps more distance in "The Unbeliever," never entering the poem and confronting the character himself as she does (in the scant disguise of a second-person "you") in "The Man-Moth." Dickinson gives her incipient unbeliever a voice, frantic and bitter. Bishop's more objective, less melodramatic words give her unbeliever not so much a voice of his own as a cautious recognizing, as if to paint and yet to protect her own unbelief, to depict it and yet to keep private—perhaps even from herself—that it is her own.

But she lets her sympathy for him show, even though, of the three allegorical voices in the poem, only the unbeliever lives in terror.

Like the cloud and the gull, he has his own delusion—that the sea is hard as diamonds and that it has a conscious will ("wants to destroy"). Yet his delusion, if not matching the reality we assume, is at least consonant with it. The sea may not be hard or want to destroy, but its fathomless softness will destroy nonetheless, and so his fear matches what by any standard he *should* fear. In that way Bishop sees to it that the unbeliever's fear makes a kind of sense. Similarly, his last words, "us all," show him as the only one of the three whose thought reaches beyond himself. Those words end the poem by encompassing and extending all the earlier voices' preoccupations. His inclusiveness makes the unbeliever's imagination more convincing, makes it less distortingly solipsistic than the cloud's and the gull's. And that his frightened imagination stands out as stronger than the others' complacent imaginations makes Bishop's sense of imagination's cost all the more terrifying. For he whose eyes stay closed sees the more truly. With eyes shut, he sees the most, and seeing the most, he fears the most. That, Bishop suggests, is imagination. Imagination, what she and her unbeliever most covet, what he risks all the past and future for, is thus what we live for—and it hurts.

It hurts less, though, in "The Man-Moth," at least in the first stanzas of that poem. There Bishop releases herself into imagination and out of its burdens by identifying with a creature that can imagine painlessly. Then, as if even that hurts her by reminding her of at what cost *she* imagines, the second half of the poem turns away from how being a Man-Moth enables some special Man-Mothian mode of mind and turns to the Man-Moth's more familiarly human fears, which are painful fears indeed.

At first, the poem invokes an urgency of place and perspective, an immediate "here" that coaxes us to identify with a world that might otherwise seem strange.

> Here, above,
> cracks in the buildings are filled with battered moonlight.
> The whole shadow of Man is only as big as his hat.
> It lies at his feet like a circle for a doll to stand on,
> and he makes an inverted pin, the point magnetized to the moon.

We naturally begin by trying to place the undefined but determining *here,* and several markers seem to help. Words like *above* and *moon-light,* especially as they follow the title's hint of an airborne per-spective, imply that we look through the Man-Moth's eyes down onto the Man. From that vertical vantage the Man's body would take up less of our view than usual and would fall in the same line of sight as his shadow, which would take up more, so that his shadow might attract the oddly large proportion of attention these lines give it. The opening of the next stanza confirms the sense that the first lines come from the Man-Moth's perspective: "But when the Man-Moth / pays his rare, although occasional, visits to the surface, / the moon looks rather different to him." He seems to visit the surface from his perch in the here above, so that the moon looks different to him from the way it looks when he lofts up high.

But then Bishop says that "He emerges / from an opening under the edge of one of the sidewalks," and suddenly we must revise the way she has made us read the perspective. The Man-Moth visits the surface from below, not from above. The moon looks different to him, not compared to how it looked before, but compared to how it looks to the Man. Only here, as the poem starts to say that the Man-Moth differs from whoever it has just been discussing, can we realize that the subject of this poem called "The Man-Moth" has, until now, been not the Man-Moth at all but merely the Man. Before, without anything to indicate otherwise, few readers are likely to think of an ordinary, pedestrian human "here" as "above." Bishop oddly mixes modes. On the one hand, she takes "here" as referring to some ordinary here, the place where the Man and all her readers walk, and so assumes some routine perspective. On the other hand, she places that here in some "above," which implies a place apart from the routine, and strangely transplants the routine to a surreal, otherworldly, Man-Mothian "below." But without some clarifying explanation, the words "here" and "above" simply do not fit together to paint the lowly world of people and pavement that Bishop calls on them to describe. Perhaps unintentionally, then, Bishop has made the opening lines seem to come from the Man-Moth's perspective, but turn out to come from the Man's. That turnabout and sudden insistence on difference force us to ask something no one is likely to have asked before reading this poem: What's the difference be-tween a Man-Moth and a Man?

Their responses to the much-fabled moon measure the differences between Man and Man-Moth. The Man lives secondarily and be-latedly. "He does not see the moon," but instead passively "observes only her vast properties." The moon's light, seen secondarily, reflected "on his hands," is "neither warm nor cold, / of a temperature impossible to record in thermometers." That is, he lives amidst the moon's effects without noticing it as a cause; and cut apart from their cause, those effects appear as pale shadows of their mysterious source (perhaps partly because a Man might know, as a Man-Moth might not, that the moon itself is no true source but rather reflects the sun's primary light). Thus, to the Man, the moon is a series of negatives, of things he does *not* do or feel or record, and "only" can "observe," indicating that he would record if he could, but he holds himself too distantly to manage even a recorder's defensively objective assimilation of the mystery. Bishop never outrightly says that the Man lives in fear, but in implicit mimicry of his tentativeness, she lets that come across even as she keeps from saying so directly. Full of a fear so pedestrian that we hardly note it as fear, the Man holds his eyes low and dares not glance at the moon.

The Man-Moth, underground, *is* low, and he too fears to glance ahigh. But from within his fear ("nervously," "trembles," "fearfully," "fears") the Man-Moth glances up, nevertheless, and follows his glance in his flight. It would be easy for him to "investigate as high as he can climb" if he felt no fear. Compared to the Man, he would then be simply foolish rather than admirably brave. But he enjoys no such earthly complacency and climbs with no false hopes. On the contrary, he is as frightened as the Man. "He thinks the moon is a small hole at the top of the sky, / proving the sky quite useless for protection." He aspires to escape through that hole, not because he lives free of fear, but instead because he fears even more than the man does. For he fears the other side of the sky will collapse on him, as the earth might cave in on his subway refuge. He thus envisions both the cosmos in general and, by implication, his personal world as susceptible to some vague but radical ruin. With a naively fussy desperation ("*quite* useless"), he wants protection from that ruin, but hardly seems likely to find it, which in turn drives him on to fear the more.

His striving, however futile, to ascend beyond fear makes him different from the Man, but it also makes him different from any moth. After all, no Man-Moth lives outside this poem, which makes

it hard to posit some more-or-less typical creature the poem is real-
istically and casually *about*. And so, when this fanciful substitute for
a creature "nervously begins to scale the faces of the buildings," he
cannot keep from suggesting allegorical comparisons to the seemingly
representative Man who begins the poem. He does not just fly high;
he flies against some figurative measure or scale of things human —
against buildings and *faces* of buildings, "man"-made things conceived and expressed through human metaphor. And he flies in a
context where to fly is to aspire. Moths never aspire; and no reader
could previously have associated aspiration with Man-Moths, having
never heard of the things before. Only people (Men, in the language
of the poem) aspire, so that the poem becomes an allegorical commentary on human ambition and the restraint of ambition by fear,
especially fear of failure. The Man dares not ascend, because he
knows he will fall; whereas the Man-Moth believes he will fall if he
dares ascend, but dares not refuse to try.

That could make him the greater fool, except for the thrill in his
daring to seek the unlikely chance, like the unbeliever. The Man-
Moth, like the unbeliever, has no access to eschatological finality,
whether it be religious, as for the unbeliever, or cosmographic (rather
than geographic), as for the Man-Moth. The Man-Moth may believe
in the other side of the sky, but he no more expects to get to what
he believes in than the unbeliever expects to get to what he doesn't
believe in. And the surely overarching voice of the poem — Bishop —
doesn't believe in the other side of the sky; she condescends comically
even to the idea of such a thing. Still, in her eager hovering over
the impossible Man-Moth, Bishop again romanticizes the unbeliever's
suspended dwelling in incompletion. The Man prematurely com-
pletes, not so much out of vanity and ignorance, like the cloud and
the gull, as out of cowardice and caution that put as severe a halt
to his imagination as the stagnant delusions of the cloud and gull.
The Man-Moth, though, sees as clearly as the Man everything that
makes the Man so timid, but he does not find the safety of caution
worth the sacrifice of imagination. He wants no riskless life. He
dwells not in the world of *have*, where live the gull and cloud and
Man, but rather in Bishop's and her unbeliever's world of *wish*.

Wish is the world — or manner of imagination — in which those
who do not believe and who do aspire will find the most that pleases
them. The world of *have* they find confining. They aspire to more

than they can have, and they cannot believe they will ever reach what they aspire to, so that only *wish* is left to fill the space between satisfaction in the here and natural, and faith in the hereafter and supernatural. Bishop thus chooses wish *instead* of belief.

Mere preference, though, does not make wish easy or pleasurable. It adds up to less than belief would add up to if she could believe. She still feels deeply uneasy about her particular fantasized wisher, the Man-Moth, for she condescendingly makes his vision of another side to the sky come across as rather silly, certainly silly compared to the fabled heights of poetic imagination. He will never reach those heights, but he has his fantasy of reaching them, and of the climactic barrier he would pass through on the way: "he climbs fearfully, thinking that this time he will manage / to push his small head through that round clean opening / and be forced through, as from a tube, in black scrolls on the light."

His willful fantasy, then, as pitiful for being a mere fantasy as it is courageous for being any fantasy at all, paradoxically includes a fantasy of resigning his will: "he will manage / to . . . be forced." Yet he imagines that crossing the threshold of natural will would suddenly catapult him to a supernatural, to a daemonic or exterior compulsion, which then, oddly enough, by forcing him into the beyond, would let him loose into his own "black scrolls on the light," into a new and grander release of his interior will.

That release of interior will sounds a lot like the two anxious events of creative contest that Bishop so elaborately figures in "The Weed," namely: birth and writing. Birth is anxious for anyone: "to push his small head through that round clean opening / and be forced through, as from a tube." But birth might be far more anxious, in retrospect, for a mythological hybrid, half one species and half another, a walking and flying emblem of bestiality whose simple being recalls a series of mythological analogues that imprint on the thought of creation a memory of violation and terror. Yet Bishop, of course, also celebrates the Man-Moth's *way* of being, especially his ultimate wish for his own creativity, which she sees not as a wish to love or to give birth (a hybrid, for one thing, might be sterile), but rather as a wish both to fly like a moth and, figuratively, to write, to leave "black scrolls on the light."

He chases that wish by flying "up the façades" of buildings, where inside, by contrast, Man stays timidly. By scaling "façades," the Man-

Moth implicitly scales illusions, or, in other words, imagination.
Ironically, he already scrolls in flight in his very quest for the outer
universe that he wants to release him into imaginative scrolling.
Seeking to do, therefore, becomes the doing. Thus, having stumbled
upon a newspaper misprint, Bishop responds to the eery and comical
allure of its hybrid idiosyncrasy by applying it to her understated
but continuous preoccupation with imagination. Her more interesting
poems, then, especially in *North & South*, are often not merely the
modest acts of visual empiricism she has grown famous for. They
also leap into allegories of imagination. After all, there *are* no Man-
Moths, no imaginary icebergs, no talking clouds or gulls, and no
meditating dead women with exploding weeds in their breasts. Instead, all those are artistic constructs—flamboyantly so, and in their
flamboyance they are implicitly about the imagination of such constructs.

Thus the Man-Moth refreshes our sense that all vision represents
a projection from within as well as a reception of some objective
without. When the Man-Moth sees the moon as a hole in the sky
or as the opening of a tube, he sees the three-dimensional as two-
dimensional, and he sees the material moon as ethereal space, and
ethereal space as a material dome or cylinder—all judging, that is,
by the Man's standards. Hence, when Bishop imagines how the Man-
Moth might see, she reimagines sight. She decontextualizes it so as
to translate or recontextualize it into an alternative empiricism independent of the habits that human empiricism takes for granted.
But with "his shadow dragging like a photographer's cloth behind
him," his sight of the moon as the end of a tube builds also on
Bishop's human vision of his likeness to a camera, a human artifact.
For the Man-Moth seems to peer down his line of sight the way a
Man might peer through the Man-Moth's mechanical likeness and
see a lens slicing the three-dimensional into the two-dimensional. In
fact, Bishop's recontextualization of vision into a Man-Mothian perspective can never be any more objective than the subjective, Man's
vision it replaces. Bishop celebrates it as the scaled façade, the illusion
we call imagination.

"(Man, standing below him, has no such illusions.)" Bishop gives
Man as a tragic and intricate contrast to her Man-Moth. Tragic,
because the illusions he holds free of still tacitly rule him: "he makes
an inverted pin, the point magnetized to the moon," though he

neither sees the moon nor has the thrill of any illusions about it. And intricate, because of the involuted way the poem reflects on Bishop herself, who in some ways is a Man and in other ways surely is not, and who is even, in some respects, more like the Man-Moth. To the extent we take Bishop as a Man, in the sense meaning person, then her little parenthetical reminder that Man has no such illusions partly disproves itself, since she gives exactly such an illusion by imagining the poem. Her parentheses, therefore, acquire an ironic and double implication. Their literal meaning complains that Man has no illusions, while at the same time their sarcastic ring tauntingly hints that Man has only foolish illusions, in contrast to the Man-Moth's bold fantasy. At the same time, of course, in other ways Bishop is a Woman and not a Man, and so can ridicule Men's dullness without implicating herself in it. She is more like the Man-Moth, imagining what he might imagine, even to her double anxiousness about his own and her own imagination. Both of them give their creative pursuits to scrolls on the light and not (so far as the poem shows about the Man-Moth) to what for most people would be the easier creation of offspring; and Bishop perhaps feels that the world's rules codify her own sexuality as hybrid or aberrant, like the Man-Moth's genealogy.[6]

Anxiousness, she implies, is the condition of imaginative ambition as well as an obstacle to it, for "what the Man-Moth fears most he must do, although / he fails, of course, and falls back scared but quite unhurt." While the Man can't wish, the Man-Moth can't help trying to translate wish into act, "thinking that this time he will manage," though he never will manage and is so clearly hopeless that Bishop says "he fails, *of course*," suggesting how inherent is failure. Together with his underground origins, the Man-Moth's dogged and futile striving combines Sysiphean repetition and Promethean determination, the drudge with the hero, the artist who depends on his failure or even, in this partly comic instance, the artist who depends on the schlemiel inside him and never gets very high except through the metaphorical height of his mere wish to get "as high as he can."

But the fundamental difference between the Man and the Man-Moth is that, like a moth, the hybrid creature of fancy will not crash back down to earth, and so he can wish without penalty and fear without inhibition. Bishop stresses that advantage by closing a stanza with the remark that he "falls back scared but quite unhurt." Yet in "The Unbeliever" she implies that any true imagination will necessarily hurt, which might reflect on the Man-Moth. A Man, it seems, will hurt upon falling, if he dares to reach a height he could fall from, and so he seldom dares at all. A moth seems much less fragile. It cannot fall. Flick at it and it merely flies away instead of falling, and so it is almost what the gull foolishly believes himself to be. A Man-Moth, in its fantastical compromise, can fly but also can fall, and can even scare, and yet cannot get hurt from falling. The Man-Moth's imagination thus remains somehow otherworldly, a rebuke to the Man's more meager daring, but still easier, because protected, and at the same time less grand, because with its protection it risks so little.

In contrast, Bishop, to aspire, must almost start from scratch by imagining unheard-of things like Man-Moths. Imagination, then, impossible for a moth, is easier for the Man-Moth, though still a struggle; tougher for the Man, who has more to lose; and perhaps tougher still for a woman who can see through the superficiality and cowardice of representative Men — those creatures who will not even look to see the moon with its aura of romance, of psychological risk, and of women. And imagination is tough especially for a woman who can see through all that and remain aware of both how she is one of those Men and also how her being at the same time different from them makes her burden double. By imagining more, she hurts more, because as an unbeliever she lets imagination lead to heights she will likely fall from.

This is, after all, a confusing and apparently a confused poem, like its mongrel title and character. It starts by seeming to talk about the Man-Moth while, it soon appears, meaning to talk about the Man. In turn, if the Man-Moth's unfragile state follows from his resemblance to and apparent ancestry from an insect, then something too accrues from his resemblance to the Man of whom he seems obscenely and impossibly bred, for a man can fall as a moth cannot. Thus the Man-Moth's falling reveals the Man taking over again from the moth, both in that he falls, and in the metaphorical sense of failure that he feels in his fall, for metaphor is the domain of men and not of moths. Indeed, it comes as no surprise that we can naturalize or explain a poem about something called a Man-Moth into an allegory about men or people. But that doesn't win our primary interest, which lies less in a curious text's susceptibility to naturalization than in its resistance to it.[7] In other words, the poem in some ways flies out of Bishop's control, not necessarily to the poem's or to her imagination's detriment, but rather in a way that makes the poem resist consistency and interpretation. In that sense it broaches the fallacy of imitative form by acting out the imaginative confusion it embodies.[8] Yet, its befuddling mimesis of disorientation partly adds to or even initiates our interest and so suggests another *kind* of poetic control, at least if we wish to associate control with artistic power itself, even if that power arises from the disruption of unity or organic form, as opposed to the more familiar New Critical or classroom dictum that art depends on unity, on weedless order. From its title to its close "The Man-Moth" forswears unity and any familiar kind of control. Instead its bisected, unheroic hero "flits" and "flutters, and cannot get aboard the silent trains / fast enough." Once he does board, then at some undecipherable speed "he travels backwards."

The discontinuity increases when Bishop says that this creature of ascension, with its yearning for progress, more habitually travels backwards, which recalls her earlier remark that his ascents are but "rare, although occasional, visits." That turns the second half of the poem back against the already turning and twisting first half. In the second half, the Man-Moth travels through a dreamy world of contracted time that oddly usurps his heroic will of the first half.

> He . . . cannot get aboard the silent trains
> fast enough to suit him. The doors close swiftly . . .
> and the train starts at once at its full, terrible speed,
> without a shift in gears or a gradation of any sort. . . .
>
>   Each night he must
> be carried through artificial tunnels and dream recurrent
>   dreams.

As in the first half, he "must" do something that he "cannot" do, but in the first half, the "must" refers to his willful action: "He must investigate as high as he can." In the second half, by contrast, the "must" refers both grammatically and emotionally to his passive submission to some exterior will: "he must / be carried." At first,

Bishop gives his incapacity in qualified form: "he fails, of course, and falls back scared *but* quite unhurt." Later, though, he simply "*cannot* get aboard" or "*cannot* tell"; things happen of themselves, to him rather than by him. The doors close themselves, the train starts at full speed without transition, as if, by the dreamy rules of some alternate ontology, time is a constant that he has joltingly caught up with, all helplessly and at once. For suddenly, the words of time are "always" and "Each night he must" and "recurrent," as opposed to the "occasional" or "visits" or "this time" of before. The frozen time freezes any hope for expansion or escape. Instead, the second half confines its surreal invention to enclosed, constraining "artificial tunnels" that sound incongruous after the soaring, skyward stretch of the first half; and so the second half grows more ordinary, as if the wild creature that once strived to fly beyond heaven now settles, defeated, for running to catch a commuter train. This more chastened Man-Moth's anxieties, no longer of their own breed, seem more like the everyday anxieties of Man, even though more intensely realized. Nor, suddenly, is the Man-Moth so alone as before:

> He does not dare look out the window,
> for the third rail, the unbroken draught of poison,
> runs there beside him. He regards it as a disease
> he has inherited the susceptibility to.

No longer daring, he fears and submits to an exterior world, whether in the unseen rail that he dramatizes into some vague but special threat, or in the inherited past, equally outside his will, that he thinks makes the rail dangerous for him. Throughout, he believes in some beyond, in the first half of the poem as a goal, and in the second half as an obstacle—so complete an obstacle that his belief in it costs him his earlier, improbable but firm belief in himself. His words echo a similar belief, late in T. S. Eliot's *The Waste Land*, in some mysterious exterior that dimly implies both a weakness within and a latent power:

> Who is the third who walks always beside you?
> When I count, there are only you and I together
> But when I look ahead up the white road
> There is always another one walking beside you

> Gliding wrapt in a brown mantle, hooded
> I do not know whether a man or a woman
> —But who is that on the other side of you?[9]

Both poems center on quest amid a deserted landscape that can hardly favor any but ironized quest, and yet they still identify with the questing they ironize. Hence the Man-Moth bravely seeks something sublimely exterior to himself and at the same time fears the ordinary all around him that he seems to fantasize into something sublimely oppressive. He tries, in the first half, to escape to aloneness, but in the second half, the populated world around him reasserts its routine.

The routine comes back so strongly that all of a sudden Bishop addresses her readers directly as if we not only could but probably will enter the Man-Moth's company, which so bursts the familiar barrier between our quotidian, readerly expectations and his eery fantasies that, at the last, the poem changes again, once more and finally deserting the world of routine for the unpredictable underworld of shadowy fable:

> If you catch him,
> hold up a flashlight to his eye. It's all dark pupil,
> an entire night itself, whose haired horizon tightens
> as he stares back, and closes up the eye. Then from the lids
> one tear, his only possession, like the bee's sting, slips.
> Slyly, he palms it, and if you're not paying attention
> he'll swallow it. However, if you watch, he'll hand it over,
> cool as from underground springs and pure enough to drink.

Until this ending, although Bishop has encouraged us to identify with the Man-Moth's heroic daring and oppressed helplessness, she has led us to identify in emotion, never in action. Then, abruptly, she addresses us as if we share the mythical world that until then she has described as apart from us and as fantastically imaginary. Where before she called forth our identification through allegorical parable and not through any sense that she referred to our world directly, now she assumes casually that we not only share the Man-Moth's world, but even that we rule it and might well capture him and violate the pristine independence she earlier presented so sympathetically. Like watchmen, we patrol the illusory world and hold it up to the cold, flashlight scrutiny of synthetic vision. The once-pitiful little Man-Moth emerges as large, with its eye big enough to shine a light in, and—in comically human words—able to "palm" or "hand over" a tear. The poem's otherworldly scale merges with our familiar scene as now we face a zoological peer, more like a criminal on the streets than an alien sprite. From the sympathetic, opening "Here" that mixes so oddly with the extraterrestrial "above" that Bishop joins it to, we change to the guarded but earthly distance of watching and disarming. By breaking our identification—and her own—with the Man-Moth, the final stanza's swerve gives a sense of conclusiveness. Perhaps Bishop then feels a guilt or regret for deserting what she had romanticized, which leads her to sentimentalize the final lines, as if to compensate. That hardly helps, for in the process she condescends to the once-wild and boldly wishful creature, reimagining him as timid and obedient.

At the end, the Man-Moth is not merely defeated by incidental circumstance; Bishop calls us in to defeat him. She envisions us as hungering for Prospero's power over Caliban. With no precedent in the poem for any such aggrandizing human will, she has us stare down the Man-Moth until he surrenders his equivalent of a bee's sting—as if we were above simply asking him. The diminished creature, at the last, can wish only surreptitiously, "slyly." Bishop seems not to realize that she imposes some wish for hegemony, apparently a projection of her own wish, onto readers she has given no cause to wish for it, and that in making us demand the Man-Moth's equivalent of a bee's sting, she makes us kill the Man-Moth she had before made us admire and pity. The poem thus begins with the cowardice of human or masculine imagination, then turns to the heroics of the Man-Moth's futile imagination, and then subdues the Man-Moth, finally sacrificing him to the feeble but prying residue of human imagination. As in "The Unbeliever," then, imagination hurts, but it is the braver response to being hurt, and so is worth the pain. At least it is worth the pain for Bishop, as she reasserts her imagination in the end, though possibly not for the finally sting-less, worse-than-castrated Man-Moth, the sad object she wreaks her chastened, hurt imagination on. But his pain, of course, cannot count in the same way, since it is the fictional pain she herself has imagined.

At the end of this poem, therefore, imagination is a beaten or—when it survives—a guilty thing. The Man-Moth's is forced underground or even killed, though killed only incidentally, while Man raids his treasure, like raiding a conquered culture's art, to supply the trumped-up museum imagination of a culture physically more powerful. The residue of human imagination is thus desperate and wishful, hanging on by its spoils, agonizingly secondary.

Indeed, a feeling of division and imaginative stagnation or strain runs through most of *North & South,* even to the doubling in its title, like the split between Man and Moth or between weed and woman. Norma Procopiow, concentrating especially on the strangely clotted and obscure love poems, sees that stagnation as acting out a confusion in Bishop's sexual identity—a likely explanation, though probably not a complete one.[10] Regardless of its sources, which probably are irrecoverably complex and multiple, that bifurcating agony over creativity and identity shows up centrally again and again in Bishop's first book.

In "The Gentleman of Shalott," she presents a man split down the middle into half man and half something else—not moth, any longer, but instead a mirrored image of the first half, making explicit "The Man-Moth" 's unspoken premise of allegory. The gentleman doesn't know which half is which, "And if half his head's reflected, / thought, he thinks, might be affected." But which side of him thinks that? He (whichever he is) can't tell, and the effort to tell can go nowhere, for he can never decipher which side does the thinking or telling, which, in turn, affects (he thinks) the thought he can't locate in the first place anyway. The question leads only to an infinite regression of thought and reflected thought, a cracked hall of mirrors that Bishop gives appropriate sound in the poem's joggling chain of imperfectly rhymed couplets and two-beat lines. Eventually the lines stretch out some as the poem caroms to a close and takes on more and more burden of explanation:

> But he's resigned
> to such economical design.
> If the glass slips
> he's in a fix—
> only one leg, etc. But
> while it stays put
> he can walk and run
> and his hands can clasp one

> another. The uncertainty
> he says he
> finds exhilarating. He loves
> that sense of constant re-adjustment.
> He wishes to be quoted as saying at present:
> "Half is enough."

He's resigned to his status, but he does not like it. It is too precarious, intriguingly like the unbeliever's, for "If the glass slips / he's in a fix." The gentleman cannot believe in any full sense of his own identity. Yet, like the unbeliever, he gets his thrill from that uncertainty. He says he finds it exhilarating, with the "he says" suggesting his defensiveness and not merely attributing the idea to him. Even Bishop's comic "etc." (like her "and so on" in line 10) cannot relieve the sense of his nervousness, which creeps forth in a flurry of qualifying words that overshadow his confidence, words like "resigned," "if . . . but," "while," "at present," and "enough." Enough, we might ask, for what?

In Tennyson's "The Lady of Shalott," the poem that Bishop's poem coyly half reflects, half is enough for art. When Tennyson's Lady seeks some second half beyond art, she loses the first half. Many readers have idealized her lonely state before she sees Lancelot and have interpreted Lancelot, with his air of adventure and the busy town, as the worldly contamination that destroys both art and the artist, the Lady. But the Lady's pristine art never fits any idealized purity, simply because of its limits: "She hath no loyal knight and true. . . . 'I am half sick of shadows,' said The Lady of Shalott."[11] She is alone while company would appeal to her; her art cuts away half her world, leaving her a remainder that seems frustratingly derivative of an original world she can never have. If her art sustained its ideal, she would never turn from it at the sound of Lancelot. The world outside her mirror may be cursed and crushing, but that does not make the world inside her mirror any better. Even the sickness of her cloistered, secondary world is only a half sickness, which looks forward to Bishop's infinite regression of mirrored uncertainty. Bishop's poem thus revises Tennyson's by parodying the Lady's state or by reinterpreting it. As in "The Unbeliever," she likes the life of tower-topped isolation, but she does not *believe* in it, she does not romanticize its ideality. Bishop points to the limits of that half world, even when its central figure strains, as her gentleman does, to deny or accommodate those limits.

Hence, when Bishop converts her character of Shalott from Tennyson's Lady to her gentleman, she reflects her fear that a lockup in the mirror world might not be, as the gentleman says, "enough." She replaces the fairy tower of protected delicacy with the casual connotation of the word "gentleman" in America a hundred years after Tennyson, where it merely suggests a man of manners; and so she gives simple finickiness where Tennyson gives a muse. The shift from Lady of Shalott to gentleman thus satirizes a fussy uncertainty that she somehow, it seems, participates in by needing to satirize, though the switch has other motives as well. It helps her complement Tennyson's poem rather than simply repeat it. It suggests a feminine pride by conspicuously foisting the silliness off on a man. And it also suggests a defensive wish simply to put the silliness off from herself, which contributes to the implication that she feels the silliness reflects on her and so she must work to deny that such silliness much matters, to deny that its preoccupations are less than "enough" for her art.

The result, as Anne Stevenson notes, is a peculiar "effect of disinterestedness," which Stevenson praises as "wholly original."[12] But is there not something frightening when Bishop makes the gentleman care or seem as if he should care about his precarious state, while she keeps a distance that will not allow her or her readers to care? Here Bishop doesn't sentimentalize form over character, in preference for some iconic literaryizing, as she almost does in "The Imaginary Iceberg." For "The Imaginary Iceberg" has no character, and "The Gentleman of Shalott" not only has a character but also gives itself over to characterizing him. She seems somehow afraid, then, to carry out what she wishes for, which balances her precariously on that wish, on the unbeliever's mast or the gentleman's mirror edge, holding emotion short of consummation, forever in the anguishing wish for a more that she doesn't quite want, because she wants most to hover in the wish for wanting more.

Such uneasy hesitation turns up frequently, especially in the less impressive of Bishop's early poems, where her formality sometimes sounds self-protective. The same reluctance, with its vague but firm sense that poetic or simply personal propriety draws some boundary, would later make her uncomfortable with the "confessional poets," who make a program of exactly the blunt address to self that Bishop's work often seems to yearn for and refuse.

All of "Cirque d'Hiver," for example, builds up to the moment of maximal wish, of greatest promise and yet also of greatest consciousness that she is not following through on that promise. The ending, then, rather than concluding, merely stops in a dramatized halt. Bishop and the toy horse face "each other rather desperately— / his eye is like a star— / we stare and say, 'Well, we have come this far.' " And there the poem stops. Abruptly, at the end, Bishop breaks the chasm between toy and person by comically elevating the toy to the realm of people and sinking the person to the realm of toys. How much is it, she makes us wonder, to have "come this far," and how far is "this far"? It might seem a considerable distance, given her efforts to make the final lines climactic. The dashes that surround the next to last line set us up to expect something special to follow it, and the analogy between eye and star hints at some onset of grand vision.[13] But then the last line finishes in a heightening of that expectation without any fulfilling of it. The poem stagnates. The toy dancer, split through the soul like so many others in Bishop's poems, nevertheless blithely dances on, oblivious to her troubles. The horse, "more intelligent" than the dancer and accustomed to carrying a burden, senses its likeness to Bishop—and then the poem ends before we can tell what that recognition leads to or if it leads to anything at all.

Bishop doesn't know whether she wants to go farther, and she protects against what might have been a brave confession by turning it into a little comic equation between toy horse and human. The amusing equation, however, may not be that comforting if her imagination falls into so mechanical a routine and needs to be wound up merely to do what does not amount to very much. "Cirque d'Hiver" is a scared poem, no more scared than "The Weed" or "The Unbeliever" or "The Man-Moth," but much less celebratory. In the major poems, fear forces an imaginative release at the same time that in other ways it imposes a terrifying confinement. But the meager comedy in lesser poems like "Cirque d'Hiver" leaves Bishop with no such compensation.

By contrast, in the much-anthologized "Roosters," Bishop rails against those who feel no stagnation and scoffs at where their haste leads. She makes the offending image specifically and comically male, and not so comically violent:

> At four o'clock
> in the gun-metal blue dark
> we hear the first crow of the first cock
>
> just below
> the gun-metal blue window
> and immediately there is an echo
>
> off in the distance,
> then one from the backyard fence,
> then one, with horrible insistence . . .

The adverb "immediately" suggests the mob urgency of violence that, in this World War II poem, Bishop makes seem unthinkingly precipitous. One cock—or army—starts up, and the others simply follow, with none of the nervous, wavering hesitation that Bishop admiringly lingers over in poems like "The Unbeliever," "The Man-Moth," and "Cirque d'Hiver." Where in those poems she identifies her own uncertainty with the poems' dawdling actors, in "Roosters" she presents herself as the victim of actors who refuse to dawdle, blaming them for their mere reflex of belief and its crowingly confident interruption of her lazy but more thoughtful and imaginative reluctance.

> Deep from protruding chests
> in green-gold medals dressed,
> planned to command and terrorize the rest,
>
> the many wives
> who lead hens' lives
> of being courted and despised;
>
> deep from raw throats
> a senseless order floats
> all over town. A rooster gloats
>
> over our beds.

Bishop resents being woken up at all, and metaphorically, she resents being woken up for war, both the proud male war of nations and decorated generals and the other male war in which—in her tellingly passive verbs—she would be woken to be courted so that she can be married and despised. The offending rooster is thus very much a cock, both behaviorally male and animally phallic, even erect:

> The crown of red
> set on your little head
> is charged with all your fighting blood.
>
> Yes, that excrescence
> makes a most virile presence,
> plus all that vulgar beauty of iridescence.

The cocks rise willy-nilly, like the weed. They do not deliberate or worry like unbelievers. Without choice, with no more than mere unthinking immediacy, they shut out the doubting hesitation that to Bishop breeds imagination and dream: "Each screaming / 'Get up! Stop dreaming!' " For Bishop, to get up *is* to stop dreaming, is to get off the unbeliever's mast and give up the Man-Moth's ambition.

Oddly, though, after berating her roosters at length, Bishop shifts modes and retells how Peter denied Jesus and then recognized his error when he heard a rooster, which thus has "come to mean forgiveness." Some readers even discuss the poem as if it ended with that happier image of belief: " 'Deny, deny, deny' / is not all the roosters cry." But Bishop's scriptural text (Matthew 26.30-75) gives Peter's denial much more attention than the bird's reminder that denial is not all. And conspicuously, the poem does not end even with that weakly defensive denial of denial, which, Bishop says, even Peter "cannot guess" the meaning of. For soon the morning light makes the poet wonder "how could the night have come to grief?" She takes the day's onset of beauty only as a reminder of the night's deserted pain. And in the final line, the rising sun, instead of appearing as some metaphor of faith in Jesus no longer denied, appears more like a metaphor of reasserted unbelief, "faithful as enemy, or friend." The morning, then, like the roosters that usher it in, makes for Bishop an emblem of wish frustrated.

Much less flamboyantly, "Chemin de Fer" (French for railroad) gives a similar emblem of frustrated wish and, more particularly, of a frustrated wish for love. The opening stanza tells us right off that the heart is at issue:

> Alone on the railroad track
> I walked with pounding heart.

> The ties were too close together
>   or maybe too far apart.

In a rhythm of uncertainty and unbelief that recalls Frost's "Neither out Far nor in Deep," Bishop punningly worries over the relation between her aloneness, with which she begins, and her connectedness, her ties. She sees the landscape as "scenery," as, in effect, a background for her own thoughts and feelings, and as "impoverished," because or, perhaps, even though she sees it as falling into ties or pairings of "scrub-pine and oak . . . mingled gray-green."

The hermit wants, even if violently, to project onto nature some vision of passionate connectedness, and Bishop seems to identify with his wish but not with his angry, roostery insistence on it:

> The hermit shot off his shot-gun
>   and the tree by his cabin shook.
> Over the pond went a ripple.
>   The pet hen went chook-chook.
>
> "Love should be put into action!"
>   screamed the old hermit.
> Across the pond an echo
>   tried and tried to confirm it.

In response to the lonely man's protesting violence, the pond merely ripples. It cares no more than the hen, who goes about her business with the usual cluck of indifference, or at most a mere ripple's worth of chiding. The two lines about the pond and the hen turn, for the only time in the poem, to single-line sentences. After the longer, enjambed rhythm of the stanza's opening vituperance, the curter sound of these lines suggests the short, chook-chooky rhythm of condescending indifference to the hermit's futile little display. He can scream that "Love should be put into action," but he seems able to act only in an unloving way, with violence and a hermit's choice to be alone.

The pond and the hen thus bear Bishop's projected rejection of the hermit's confidence. The pond "tried and tried to confirm" the hermit's belief, and so does Bishop, she implies. She wishes she were like the scrub-pine unanxiously with the oak or the gray unworriedly mingling with the green, but she cannot believe she ever will be. Instead, she remains "Alone on the railroad track," tied inflexibly

into its iron way, protectively resorting—as elsewhere in *North &
South*—to the uneasy distance that a title in French can inflict on
a poem in English, especially in a poem that, like others with French
titles or settings ("Quai d'Orleans," "Sleeping on the Ceiling," "Cirque d'Hiver"), addresses love in a haltingly formal prosody. The
hesitant formality, here as in so many Bishop poems, indicates that
this usually shy poet, who chose to pass most of her writing life far
from the centers of publicity and publication, feels somehow ill at
ease, perhaps with her wishes themselves, and more certainly with
the nakedness her wishes take on when proclaimed in the public
arena of poetry and print.

Rarely, she musters a more confident vision of wish. "The Monument" begins with fussy uncertainty, with Bishop's habit of or
insistence on publicly changing her mind and advertising her uncertainty: "Now can you see the monument? It is of wood / built
somewhat like a box. No. Built / like several boxes. . . ." Her thought
here seems simply the thought of its own moment, of "Now." But
she concludes the poem more assertively, with an emblem of the
imaginative wish that dominates *North & South:*

> It is an artifact. . . .
> The monument's an object, yet those decorations . . .
> give it away as having life, and wishing. . . .
> It may be solid, may be hollow.
> The bones of the artist-prince may be inside
> or far away on even drier soil.
> But roughly but adequately it can shelter
> what is within (which after all
> cannot have been intended to be seen).
> It is the beginning of a painting,
> a piece of sculpture, or poem, or monument,
> and all of wood. Watch it closely.

Here Bishop takes up a low Stevensian mode, mixing Wallace Stevens's pontificating about imagination with her own more straightforward, even skeptical details. She bluntly includes an unimpressed,
questioning voice that sees the monument as little more than refuse:
" 'It's piled-up boxes, / outlined with shoddy fret-work, half-fallen
off, / cracked and unpainted. It looks old.' " She acknowledges the
impulse that generates her monument as rough or merely adequate,

but against that skeptical voice she still sees the monument as a wedding of life and wish, an icon of imagination, of something that can grow. Nailed together of clumsy wood, it may lack the sleek finish of a polished alloy, but it is organic, like the weed, and she even treats it as if it were still alive, suggesting that, as in "The Weed," some hidden power within will grow of its own will or its own embodiment of some earlier artist's wish. In "The Weed," that release of power catches her unprepared. Here she gladly expects and predicts it, perhaps because she makes art itself directly her subject. Poems begin in wish, Bishop suggests, so that her monument images wish's unfoldable power, the beginning that we can watch with more pleasure in the process it sets going than we might find even in its eventual finish.

Thus, as in "Cirque d'Hiver," "The Monument" ends with its focus on some beyond that it promises will follow. But "Cirque d'Hiver" suddenly stops, with no sound of confidence that the promise will surpass the wish or even that it will ever come at all. Here there seems no doubt it will come, for only that confidence justifies the preoccupation with beginnings that by themselves look a little shoddy. And so she ends the poem with the certainty of imperative. "Watch it closely," because it will grow into something special.

In the middle of "The Map," Bishop proclaims a similar and, in some ways, still stronger confidence, for she describes not just an emblem of imaginative promise, like the monument, but actually a map to the mind's hidden treasure, a genie's lamp, in effect, that she can caress into granting imagination's wish:

> We can stroke these lovely bays,
> under a glass as if they were expected to blossom....
> These peninsulas take the water between thumb and finger
> like women feeling for the smoothness of yard-goods.

Here, in the most confident moment of what is, as we have seen, a not altogether confident poem, Bishop coaxes imagination out of geography, not because she believes it lies there latently in waiting—for after all, bays will never blossom on a map—but because we can summon it by assertion. The power lies not in the mapped geography so much as in the mapping of geography. The peninsulas do not finger the water, but her likening them to women shopping or browsing suggests a primacy of human and maybe of feminine control and choice. Wish, these lines imply, can be fulfilled by an exertion of care and will.

Elsewhere, though, the more assured poems of *North & South* rely on a confidence that seems fearful, on a trumped-up or merely wished-for cheer that defends against some larger threat and so apologizes or pleads for confidence. Perhaps many readers would take "The Fish," one of Bishop's most admired poems, as her most conclusively confident poem. There she catches a "tremendous fish" and surveys it closely in one of the finest of those precise descriptions she is famous for. Then, she says, "I stared and stared / and victory filled up / the little rented boat," "until," in the poem's final words, "everything / was rainbow, rainbow, rainbow! / And I let the fish go." Here suddenly she catches what she wished for, and so no longer needs to wish. To preserve the edge of wish, then, she must give up what she has, so she can have again more truly by not having. It recalls Faulkner's claim that Hemingway failed by sticking to what he already knew he could succeed at, instead of daring the failures that, by overreaching, make the truest success.[14] On the other hand, Bishop does not sound convinced that she really gains that much by catching her fish. For her cheerily sentimental word "rainbow," with its repetition that, rather than giving emphasis, only enhances the sense that she feels the word's inadequacy, together with the sudden exclamation point and its redoubled effect of straining too hard at the end of what had remained an understated, calm poem, all seem to compensate for some fear of ordinariness in her understatement and quiet. Her letting the fish go, dramatized by putting it all in the final words, seems too willfully a striving for conclusive wisdom. She can throw the fish back, if she likes, but to gloat over throwing it back sounds too easily superior, since most of us, rather than throwing fish back, enjoy eating them now and then. Instead of ending with a wish for something to say, she seems not to know how to end, and so she goes, in effect, fishing for profundity, violating at the end the modesty and indirection that she was to win such admiration for.[15]

"A Miracle for Breakfast" similarly speaks with a confidence in excess of what its subject calls for. It is outrightly about wish, about a starving man's plea for food. But it works so hard to make something Parisian and formally *au courant* (a sestina) that the direness of his suffering almost disappears in the cheery dance steps of form. The crumb that should evoke our pity at its paltriness seems so exaggeratedly farfetched, even as a metaphor of meager charity, that it survives mainly as the object of a sestina's arbitrary play.[16] But a sestina is a handy thing for a hungry poet. If you don't know what to say, then if only you can get it started, the form will go a long way to guide you to the rest of the poem. Thus Pound revived the sestina in the midst of his eclectic and often imitative struggle to find his own form and voice. But Pound's famous "Sestina: Altaforte" (1909) brilliantly aligns the obsessiveness of sestina form with the several obsessions of his narrating voice, Bertran de Born. Bishop's voice in "A Miracle for Breakfast" never takes on such power or distinctiveness or so close a relation to the form. An American poem that begins with people waiting, in Paris no less, for coffee "to be served from a certain balcony, / —like kings of old," hardly suggests very clearly that those who wait are to be pitied for starvation. The tone obscures the subject, and makes it seem that the subject doesn't really interest her. She has a wish for a poem, but not a subject for one.

In other poems, Bishop chooses titles like "Little Exercise" and "Large Bad Picture" that apologize right from the start that she doesn't have a subject as strong as her wish to make a poem. "Little Exercise" commands an act of wishful unbelief; it directs us to "think" a series of scenes, as opposed to just presenting those scenes straightforwardly in the usual guise of suspended disbelief. The final stanza imagines—or asks us to imagine—someone oddly relaxed for the poet of "The Weed," "The Unbeliever," and "The Man-Moth": "Think of someone sleeping in the bottom of a row-boat / tied to a mangrove root or the pile of a bridge; / think of him as uninjured, barely disturbed." Such a sleeper would make almost a reverse unbeliever. Like the unbeliever, he closes his eyes over water, but he rests low and horizontally, not high and vertically, and he sleeps safely, remaining calm and calculatedly immovable. Bishop, though, stresses that she does not believe in him; he is to be thought of, that is, to be imagined and not seen. He is her unbelieving dream of belief, a mere exercise, and a little one at that. She does not have, or at least does not show that she has, a strong enough occasion for the poem to justify it to her readers (the epigraph, *"To Thomas*

Edward Wanning," suggests a private occasion); and she confesses her lack in the title, as if in hope that recognizing the weakness will give the poem some saving rationale in self-consciousness.

One critic thinks that such self-conscious apologizing makes the center of interest in "Large Bad Picture." Penelope Laurans finds a roughness and naiveté there that she defends as appropriately mimicking the picture's failure. She does not make clear how she can tell purposefully, ironically bad poetry from just plain bad poetry.[17] Still, even if we cannot tell whether the undistinguished verse is deliberately undistinguished—and it is not clear it would help if we could—what Laurans says about the rough prosody surely holds for the embarrassed title, which again sounds like an apology for the forced occasion of the poem. In "Large Bad Picture," Bishop tries to make her own art and to displace her fear of that art's weakness onto its object, the picture. But her effort to displace the blame reinforces the sense that she strains to poeticize whatever is handy, the sense of faintly imagined motive to write the poem, as when a weak writer tries to compensate by putting poorly chosen words in quotation marks instead of by choosing stronger words. Rather than apologizing for what she writes about, Bishop needs to write about something that needs no apology.

We can see, then, part of the reason she later writes about places that her readers will think of as exotic, as inherently worthy of her imagination's rendering and commentary; and such places will dominate her next two books. Already, as she writes the later poems of *North & South*, Bishop has moved her home to Key West, archetypally a kind of geographical edge, and begun to set poems there, including, in whole or part (in sequence of publication), "Late Air,"[18] "Florida," "The Fish," "Roosters," "Jerónimo's House," "Cootchie," "Seascape," and "Little Exercise." As yet, however, she struggles more with her wish for poems and reasons to write them, with the occasions of poems, than with place as in itself an occasion. She especially struggles with that wish for imagination in a story called "The Sea & Its Shore," published in 1937, when she had written about a fourth of the poems in *North & South*.

"The Sea & Its Shore" tells how Edwin Boomer gathers the litter off the beach every evening, pausing to read the trash before igniting his nightly bonfire. His reading grows obsessive:

> Edwin Boomer lived the most literary life possible. No poet, novelist,

or critic, even one who bends over his desk for eight hours a day, could imagine the intensity of his concentration on the life of letters.

His head, in the small cloud of light made by his lantern, was constantly bent forward, while his eyes searched the sand, or studied the pages and fragments of paper that he found.

He read constantly. His shoulders were rounded, and he had been forced to start wearing glasses shortly after undertaking his duties.[19]

Boomer oddly takes on the aura of a belated poet so preoccupied with reading that the things already written usurp or at least radically compromise the would-be poet's imaginative vision. Yet even as she worries over the intimidations of high literacy, Bishop belittles "literary life" by not taking it seriously, by comparing it to the obsessive reading of trash and joking that the people who presume they lead a "life of letters" do not really go at it so hard — "even one" who works hard works no longer than the ordinary worker's goal of an eight-hour day (not yet standard in 1937). Boomer's commitment reaches much beyond that. He not only redefines the bounds of literature and of what we have since come to call textuality, he altogether removes any limits: "The world, the whole world he saw, came before many years to seem printed, too" (178).

But unlike a structuralist of thirty or forty years later, who sees and usually even celebrates omnipresent textuality as inherent, Boomer rebels against the textuality that fascinates him. "Our presses turn out too much paper covered with print" (172), he thinks. It would not matter that too much has been written unless that plenitude somehow threatened him. Implicitly, Bishop feels the past as a burden, as competition that does what she might otherwise have done first and hence condemns her to secondariness. Boomer's name echoes the name (Bulmer) of the grandparents who raised Bishop for that brief but formative time that she pays the most attention to in her memoirs and stories,[20] so that he represents both herself and the past against which she defines herself. Boomer enacts her resentment against the past. He stabs the printed papers with the nail on his staff, and "Sometimes he would put a match to this file of papers and walk along with it upraised like a torch, as if they were his paid bills" (173). Somehow, burning history does more than just erase the past. It also makes him feel he has paid his debt to the past. It thus both denies and acknowledges history in the same way Derrida will deny or submit to erasure a term or concept that he nevertheless goes on using. Bishop's rebellion against the past is therefore complicated and perhaps duplicitous, yet still absolute:

> But the point was that everything had to be burned at last. All, all had to be burned, even bewildering scraps that he had carried with him for weeks or months. Burning paper was his occupation, by which he made his living, but over and above that, he could not allow his pockets to become too full, or his house to become littered.
>
> Although he enjoyed the fire, Edwin Boomer did not enjoy its inevitability. (179-80)

He enjoys the freedom in destroying, and so releasing himself from, the past, but resents that he cannot freely choose that destruction. He resents that even his destruction of the past is willed by the past he destroys, whether by the historical demands of his occupation or by the written words themselves, which somehow call to be burned.

Ironically, the writing he burns for his freedom flies up into the sky in a way that suggests it is itself free. A bird, he notes, flies according to "long tradition, by a desire that could often be understood to reach some place or obtain some thing," even if only, sometimes, "for show." "But the papers," when they fly in the wind, "had no discernible goal, no brain, no feeling of race or group. They soared up, fell down, could not decide, hesitated, subsided, flew straight to their doom in the sea, or turned over in midair to collapse on the sand. . . . They were not proud of their tricks, either, but seemed unconscious of the bravery, the ignorance they displayed, and of Boomer, waiting to catch them on the sharpened nail" (174). Such records of the past taunt poor burdened Boomer, because they carry a tradition for Boomer and for Bishop, but they follow no tradition themselves. They have no will, no goal or purpose, no pride or knowledge or consciousness, but they transmit all those things to Boomer and Bishop and all of us who read Bishop's story or a commentary on it. When the past burdens us with envy, it seems to have had a freedom not just that we lack, but that we lack because the seemingly free past denies it to us, reinforcing our envy in a vicious cycle. The past, of course, never had such freedom, for to itself it was always present. Freedom is only the present's projection, from Boomer or Bishop or any of us, onto the past: "To Boomer's drunken vision the letters appeared to fly from the pages. He raised his lantern and staff and ran waving his arms, headlines and sentences streaming around him" (175). This is "The Map" turned nightmare, because the mapmaker-artist's freedom so loosens itself as to apply no longer to the visionary imagination of the mapmaker-artist but now to his actual tools, in a kind of Pirandello or Pinocchio or Nutcracker Suite fantasy of the artist's independence gone awry.

In "The Map," the effect is much happier:

> The names of seashore towns run out to sea,
> the names of cities cross the neighboring mountains
> —the printer here experiencing the same excitement
> as when emotion too far exceeds its cause.

But unlike in "The Map," in "The Sea & Its Shore" we concentrate less on the artist than on the audience. We never see Boomer write; we only see him obsessively read. The independence of language comes not, as in "The Map," from some celebratable overreaching of artistic exuberance. It is a more thorough and more threatening independence, for the language escapes the artist's will altogether. The whole world has become language, and just goes on its random way, not even resisting the artist's will, for it is so free it hasn't any will at all, neither for opposition nor for anything else. It thus renders the artist irrelevant, which may have to do with Boomer's odd way of seeming to stand in for Bishop's anxiety about her role as artist even though he never produces anything himself.

That gives Boomer plenty of motive to burn the past and to burn the language he reads, for only by repression can he win any freedom. The reading he picks out as applying in particular to him urges him to seclude " 'himself from all friends and acquaintances' " and " 'abide in all possible privacy' " so that he can " 'use his natural faculties more freely in diligently searching for that he so much desires' " (176). Here is a man under threat. He cannot simply do what he wants. Contact with any larger world than himself, he imagines, will erode himself. Such a perspective permits no traditionally unanxious view of writers' relation to their literary past. They will not be the happy students of their predecessors, carefully picking out whoever most interests them and applying what they learn to advance literature, as if literature moved along in a cumulative and more or less linear progression in the—by comparison—innocent way we imagine the growth of science or technology or mathematics. That would take belief; it would take the acceptance of a common, positivist, even prescribable set of goals and standards for literature. But in literature, we value surprises, even unpredictability. The literature we can predict is the literature we already have. For Boomer and Bishop, then, literature is a system of unbelief.

By contrast, the newspaper fragment that Boomer picks out as unrelated to himself describes a believer: " 'She slept about two hours and returned to her place in the hole, carrying with her an American flag, which she placed beside her. Her husband has brought her meals out to her and she announced that she intends to sit in the hole until the Public Social Service Company abandons the idea of setting a pole there' " (176). This believer has none of Boomer's doubt or fear. She is a patriot; she puts trust in a supportive husband, a continuously affirmed connection to others around her; and she knows she will win. Instead of sitting, eyes closed, atop a pole she can fall from at any moment, like the unbeliever, she sits only when awake, with her eyes open, down in the hole for a future pole, where it is impossible to fall. Such self-confidence, to Bishop, seems worth no more than parody.

Boomer and Bishop find far more troubling the scraps of print "that fascinated but puzzled" (176), that might apply to him or might not. The longest of those directly addresses the issue of a writer's self-confidence:

> "I couldn't send in my lesson although I am thinking of being able to write like all the Authors, for I believe that is more in my mind than any other kind of work. . . .
>
> "Mr. Margolies, I am thinking of how those Authors write such long stories of 60,000 or 100,000 words in those magazines, and where do they get their imagination and the material.
>
> "I would be very pleased to write such stories as those Writers."
>
> Although Boomer had no such childish desire, he felt that the question posed was one having something to do with his own way of life; it might almost be addressed to him as well as to the unknown Mr. Margolies. (177)

The naive correspondent for a writing course (one Jimmy O'Shea of Fall River, as we know from Bishop's delightful "The U.S.A. School of Writing," published posthumously and apparently written some thirty years after "The Sea & Its Shore"[21]) speaks bluntly — without

Bishop's or even Boomer's sophistication—what both Boomer and Bishop implicitly feel: They want to imagine anew, as other writers have, but somehow they cannot do what the other writers did, as if the room to imagine has already been taken by those who came before them.

At that point, though, Boomer and Bishop start to differ, for Bishop, after all, imagines Boomer, and hence obliquely imagines something new out of her feeling that she cannot imagine anything new. Boomer disavows such desire as childish, but he recognizes that it matters to him, that somehow the question points at him as surely as it points at Mr. Margolies. And Mr. Margolies, we know from "The U.S.A. School of Writing," is Bishop herself working under an assumed name as a correspondence school writing teacher. Thus someone (Mr. O'Shea) writes Bishop to ask how writers write, because he wants urgently to write too. Then Boomer, struggling to read so hard that he does not even know he really wants to write, finds the sadly cast-off letter and recognizes himself in the addressee more than in the addressor. That shows him trying to identify with the position of power in this particular exchange when we can see he really is at least as much like the poor simpleton who writes the letter.

Meanwhile, Bishop, trying to stay outside this buffoon's economy of frustration, distances herself from it both by reminding herself that she is the authoritative Mr. Margolies whom people refer such problems to and by writing this story that flaunts her authorship, allowing her both to gain and to sustain that authority. But at the same time, the very subject she chooses to write about throws into relief her preoccupation with the tenuousness of writerly authority, and her authority as Mr. Margolies is of course a fraud. Just as Boomer would like to think that the letter to Mr. Margolies doesn't apply to Boomer, so Bishop would like to think that the parable of Boomer doesn't apply to Bishop. But of course in each case they do apply.

In this way, Bishop senses in "The Sea & Its Shore" that writing is omnipresent and yet still feels secondary. It is a metaphor or questing for originality, for impossible escape from belatedness and into the wish for a new version of some romanticized and lost primality, a time before writing or a time of the original writing, a time, however, that no written culture can really imagine in the first place. The story's final sentence quietly agonizes over her struggle to acknowledge the past and her fear of repeating it, over the urgency of newness and its impossibility: "It is an extremely picturesque scene, in some ways like a Rembrandt, but in many ways not" (180). That same agony comes across extraordinarily in a letter Bishop sent Marianne Moore:

> This morning I have been working on THE SEA & ITS SHORE— or rather, making use of your and your mother's work—and I am suddenly afraid that at the end I have stolen something from THE FRIGATE PELICAN. I say: "Large flakes of blackened paper, still sparkling red at the edges, flew into the sky. While his eyes could follow them, he had never seen such clever, quivering manoeuvres." It was not until I began seeing pelicans that my true source occurred to me. I know you speak of the flight like "charred paper", and use the word manoeuvres. I am afraid it is almost criminal. I haven't the book here and I wonder if you will tell me just how guilty I am and forgive what was really unconscious. When I think of the care and time that you and your mother have taken with that poor story. . . . I have taken over, or gobbled up like a pelican, everything you suggested except one: "It is an extremely picturesque scene. . . ." You say you feel it to be too "automatic". In a way, that was what I meant it to be—I was, I suppose, making fun of an automatic reaction to the scene I was describing and I wanted, as the only "moral" to the story, to contradict, as quietly as possible, the automatic, banal thing that one might have said: "How *picturesque*—He looks like a Rembrandt!" That is, the conclusion of the sentence, "but in many ways not" is really thought of as being spoken in a different tone of voice. However, if this over-subtlety (and I'm afraid, superiority) on my part did not make itself plain to you there must be something very wrong and I'm going to try to change it.[22]

Bishop sounds stunningly anxious at the thought that she may have slipped into acting like her character Boomer, a reader, rather than like her chosen self-characterization as author. She is wrong to recall the word "manoeuvres" in Moore's "The Frigate Pelican"; and though Moore's poem does use the phrase "charred paper," Bishop never changed her own phrasing, neither about the paper nor in the final sentence that refers to Rembrandt and then defensively retracts the reference. In the same way, she worries over her connection to Moore in the letter and then, by keeping the story as it was, retracts the worry.

With all the uncertainty implicit in "The Sea & Its Shore," especially uncertainty about the power of the self and of the self's literary or poetic imagination, Bishop's fretting over the possibility that she has unconsciously imitated Moore represses or obscures a deeper source or a threateningly closer analogy in Whitman's "As I Ebb'd with the Ocean of Life," the great American crisis poem of poetic confidence, which similarly places the poet on the seashore amidst the trash of human imagination.

I too but signify at the utmost a little wash'd-up drift. . . .

Oppress'd with myself that I have dared to open my mouth,
Aware now that amid all that blab whose echoes recoil upon me I
  have not once had the least idea who or what I am,
But that before all my arrogant poems the real Me stands yet untouch'd,
  untold, altogether unreach'd,
Withdrawn far, mocking me with mock-congratulatory signs and bows,
With peals of distant ironical laughter at every word I have written,
Pointing in silence to these songs, and then to the sand beneath.[23]

Whitman cries out—or realizes—that he and his works are no more than trash, and that even the trashy self that he now belatedly discovers fails to evoke "who or what I am," the "real Me" that remains beyond his language and even looks down at it, ridiculing his triumphs of language as no more than the trash, sand, and trashy poems that his dreamed-up self has foolishly mistaken for the real self. Whitman is blunter than Bishop—he scorns his own writing, whereas she has Boomer scorn other people's writing for her—and perhaps in some ways he is less evocative in tone, but the struggle is much the same. Each realizes that nothing he or she can write will ever satisfy, that no common language—which is to say, no language at all—will ever evoke those furthest fantasies of independent or unique selfhood that, in this Romantic or post-Romantic age, drive us to produce literature in the first place. And each tries to defeat the impossibility of making a new literature by trying to make a literature that centers on the recognition of that impossibility. Whitman screams and whispers and pleads his dilemma. He is the personalist and melodramatist, where Bishop remains so indirect that almost no one has commented on their similarity of preoccupation or even addressed her work in the terms of crisis that seem inevitable for Whitman.[24] Nina Baym notes the tendency for critics and theorists of American literature to read works by men in terms of crisis and yet to remain blind both to contrasting and to similar patterns of crisis in works by women.[25] In Bishop's case, the blindness is almost partly her own, in a sort of subversive defense against the patriarchal world's blindness, suggesting through delicacy of tone and indirectness of perspective what Whitman orates and sings out in ostensibly his own voice.

Yet to put it that way places Whitman at some culturally masculine norm of direct proclamation from which Bishop's more culturally feminine norm derives in a restrictively secondary way. Such is how readers have generally approached the task of characterizing Bishop's manner. But a comparison to Whitman's self-declared barbarism makes Bishop seem secondary only if we forget, as Whitman often pleads with us and with himself to forget, that his "barbaric yawp" is every bit as defensive as Bishop's acculturated civilization and good manners. For Whitman's point in "As I Ebb'd with the Ocean of Life" is "that before all my arrogant poems the real Me stands yet untouch'd, untold, altogether unreach'd, / Withdrawn far." The very terms of our language, or perhaps more of our culture than of our lexicon, terms like *direct* (such as for Whitman) and *indirect* (such as for Bishop, especially when set against the likes of Whitman) suggest for the Whitmanian and usually masculine poet a centrality and primacy that assumes a confident, absolute, positivist sense of self, one that Saussure's notions of semiotic profusion or Derrida's exposure of the myth of voice might make us reject. But though Derrida can give us useful terms and a fuller understanding, we do not need Derrida for the point, for it is already Whitman's point.

Whitman's directness, what he calls here his arrogance, is not really any more direct or central or primary than Bishop's indirectness. Neither poet can reach or believe in a true or transcendent self. Both are unbelievers. But Whitman forever oscillates between, on the one hand, the private apocalypse of unbelief, as in "As I Ebb'd," or in the terrified eruptions he buries in the middle of "Song of Myself" (such as section 28), and, on the other hand, the public arias and orations of belief—partly sincere, partly comical, and partly a desperate prop against the inner resurgings of doubt. Whitman, in other words, is often as much the unbeliever as Bishop, but most of the time he *pretends* to believe. Hence his very directness is an indirection, a terrified bulwark against doubt. Which, in turn, makes Bishop's caution and hesitance, in some respects, a greater directness, a greater honesty, than Whitman's bombast. The point is not to measure and, least of all, to judge either poet against some scale of directness, but rather to explore how our preconceptions about such habits of measuring and privileging can lead us both to underestimate the achievement of a poet like Bishop, and, simply, to misread her.

In some sense, nevertheless, that would imply that she herself joins in the misreading, if her increasing search for some special exterior place to write about comes across as compensating for a frustrated sense of insufficient interior place, of failed self. But the sense of interior failure, I am suggesting, is not tied specifically to indirection so much as to the state of post-Romantic poetry itself—which tends, like Modern literature more generally, toward elaboration, toward indirection, whether in Whitman's way, Bishop's way, or some other way. And having recognized and canonized the intricate mazings of Modern literature, scholars increasingly and, by now, even ritually find versions of those same complications in earlier literature, encouraging the notion that literature and all art are inherently and even definingly acts of indirection, of unbelief—a notion encouraged and extended still more by Structuralist and post-Structuralist privileging of sign and writing over the signified and transcendent.

All this suggests that Bishop's quest for some exotic geography of subject, for a place to write about that can justify a wish to write, a wish that somehow refuses to justify itself, doesn't so much reveal a failure of imagination as it exposes an inevitable condition of imagination, a limitless deferral (like Derrida's *différance*). She feels some default of grandeur in the self—as any post-Romantic writer intimidated by the preemptions of tradition will —and tries to recoup that loss by making it in itself her subject. That works, but it hurts, and if she keeps repeating it she would canonize herself, turn her own self—her early poems of struggle—into part of the tradition that restricts her room for newness. And so she moves to something different, something outside the self, or something that she can imagine lies outside the self. She thus moves to a preoccupation with place, not so differently from the classic pattern of poets who begin in lyric, whether out of youthful exuberance or because they follow the Virgilian, Miltonic model, and then move, if not to epic, then at least to a more national or public poetry, less openly narcissistic and more assertively cultural. Bishop even became poetry consultant to the Library of Congress and, almost as if dutifully, produced a poem called "View of the Capitol from the Library of Congress." But her increasing preoccupation with place in her second and third books continues the sense of dissatisfaction with self in her first book. She simply starts to look for the compensations less in the self and more in the world around the self, onto which she can project the self and then, through that indirection, sometimes see the self more clearly. Either way, whether she looks inside or looks outside, Bishop doesn't believe in what she sees.

She sounds, then, much like her lighthouse at the end of "Seascape," a witty and powerfully anxious poem that concludes in distant echo of yet another musing over the edge, another seashore poem, Wallace Stevens's "The Idea of Order at Key West." At Key West, when the day begins, the roosters impose "deep from raw throats / a senseless order... / all over town" ("Roosters"). Such violence is hardly the order of Stevens's "ghostlier demarcations, keener sounds."[26] Day brings the clarity of its diffused light, and Bishop the unbeliever distrusts clarity. The lighthouse, like Bishop, oddly makes a kind of confidence of its self-doubt. It "will remember," she says, mixing a word that refers to the future with a word that refers to the past. It believes, in other words, that in the future it will recover the day's present as the night's past, but its belief about its future power comes in the form of an unbelief about its present power. Bishop chooses to write about the lighthouse when its light is off, when its power is potential and latent rather than active or kinetic. She will not celebrate the full-fledged thing.

Instead, she celebrates its anticipation. The Man-Moth flies high— and falls. She could end her poem with the Man-Moth rising high in hope, but she deserts his hope halfway through the poem and turns to his surreptitious wanderings underground. She might have ended there, but suddenly she brings in some urban spelunker who oddly defies the timidity and willful oblivion the poem had earlier associated with ordinary Man. She fractures her sympathies, which had rested so largely with the Man-Moth, and sends after the elusive creature, as we have seen, some part of her own Man-Mothian curiosity defensively masked under a suddenly intruding "you":

> If you catch him,
> hold up a flashlight to his eye. It's all dark pupil,
> an entire night itself, whose haired horizon tightens
> as he stares back, and closes up the eye. Then from the lids
> one tear, his only possession, like the bee's sting, slips.

These two sides of Bishop's psychic investment join in the lighthouse of "Seascape," which in an architectural metaphor of shyness and boldness repeats both the Man-Moth's covert cryings in the night and the human explorer's prying into the frightened creature's benighted retreat. Neither side has much confidence in itself. The Man-Moth slinks off to a lonely refuge while the human skeptic casts outside the self in search of some authenticating purity of unspoiled exotica, as Bishop will travel beyond her homelands in search of a place that can lend her some inherent genuineness, some authenticity she can know rather than one she must forever prove.

But no one will ever reach the authenticating origin of human imagination. The very act of imagination presupposes some displacement (*différance*) from an original that the same displacement defies. When it gets dark, the lighthouse will remember. Then, in the dark, he (as Bishop calls the lighthouse) will try to expose the futility of light that he cannot express except through a memory in the dark. The darkness, then, depends for its supposedly reassuring expressiveness on the memory of an inexpressiveness, which in turn defines itself by its nervous impatience to be remembered—but what is to be remembered if the past, the origin, is itself only a blank anticipation of the future that remembers it? Nothing. And yet, there at the edge of the sea, at the line of ghostlier demarcation, we have the poem, born, then, from the very wish for a poem, rather than from any representation of an authentic place. For, as "The Map" tells us, the mapmaker's wish overpowers the conformations of land and water.

Still, no mapmaker, no poet, can summon and dismiss wish at will. In "The Weed," Bishop discovers with a compound of horror and delight that imagination can sprout from inside her mind and outside her will. The interior frightens Bishop, even when her fear of it releases her imagination. And so, after her first book, instead of believing in what that book shows rankling inside her, Bishop turns to poems of the exterior, poems of external place, onto which she can displace the eruption inside, and thus perhaps recover it in reassuringly safer and more public form.

CHAPTER THREE

Where: *A Cold Spring, Questions of Travel*

> Should we have stayed at home and thought of here?
> . . . .
> What childishness is it that while there's a breath of life
> in our bodies, we are determined to rush
> to see the sun the other way around?
>
> —"Questions of Travel"

Bishop travels. She writes about the places she travels to, but not with the bragging of, say, a Hemingway, not with any assurance— not even a trumped-up assurance like Hemingway's—that her voyaging needs no justification. To Bishop, one place seems always the evasion of another place. She concludes "Questions of Travel" by thinking of a

> sudden golden silence
> in which the traveller takes a notebook, writes:

> *"Is it lack of imagination that makes us come*
> *to imagined places, not just stay at home?*
> *Or could Pascal have been not entirely right*
> *about just sitting quietly in one's room?*

> *Continent, city, country, society:*
> *the choice is never wide and never free.*
> *And here, or there . . . No. Should we have stayed at home,*
> *wherever that may be?"*

The traveler travels not simply to places unseen before, nor even, in any inherent sense, to actual places, but instead to imagined places, places anticipated by a mythology of exotica, whereby we assign to other locales a special status of difference that corrals them outside ourselves. We cast them apart from us to bolster some romanticizing of our own distinctiveness. But any such outcasting grows out of a highly conflicted wish (as Bishop would later suggest in "In the Waiting Room"), because we also press them away to cast from ourselves a threatening sense of identification with the foreign. Against that threat, an ideology of exotica lets us imagine that the things we share with other peoples were never a part of ourselves in the first place. To expel and confine the threatening likenesses and differences helps us forget that by some scales we do not see or refuse to see, the things we reject and feel attracted to as foreign might seem in some critical way our own.

But "the choice is never wide and never free."[1] We can never keep wholly to ourselves or even to a fiction of ourselves, from which it follows that only with caprice can we draw a confident boundary between what we label as our own world and what we label as another world. Thus it could not make sense to answer "yes" to Bishop's question of travel, for if the places we go to are imagined then it cannot be a lack of imagination that urges us to them. And so she answers "No." But strangely she follows her answer with another, and this time, a concluding question, or a sentence that, by closing with a question, partly prevents conclusion. Her final question clarifies why Bishop denies Pascal's ascetic wish to minimize external worldliness. We shouldn't simply stay at home, because we *can't* stay at home—we don't even know the boundary between original and belated that would separate home from travel. We don't know what home is.

Bishop especially doesn't know what home is. Aside from her point that none of us knows the boundaries of home, she in particular sees more easily through our commonplace confidence in an illusory idea of home, because no such confidence ever came to her, shunted around as she was in early childhood between cities and parental figures and countries, and separated from a mother she for a while believed (however uncertainly and fearfully) would return to her, and who did return, only and traumatically to leave again both in

place and in mind.² It matters, then, that Bishop calls our attention
to how she builds her public poem out of a private notebook. Much
as she implies a general principle, that no one can have a pure sense
of home, she nevertheless colors it with her own palette of nuance.
These are, after all, finicky, nervous lines, though with none of the
playful, half-mock finickiness of "Filling Station." She feels some
need to prop up her own imagination's defense by setting it against
a powerful precursor (Pascal), and even then she poses it question-
ingly, as she does again in the poem's final sentence, and all in the
prissy-sounding context of a complaint that if we didn't travel, then
"surely it would have been a pity." This is not to suggest that Bishop
is wrong to say it would be a pity if we didn't travel. It is simply
to suggest that her questioning here images an uncertainty that, in
this poem, she lets confine her imagination, as opposed to the questions that conclude "Filling Station" or Frost's "Design" with such
reverberating expansion.

"Questions of Travel" thus sounds strangely blunt and nervous.
More forthrightly than her other poems, it poses the questions that
dominate the large middle of Bishop's career, the years she was most
preoccupied with travel and place. Bishop sees that travel cannot
be an innocent act. It must be questioned. It doesn't present us with
an inert place. On the contrary, it is travel to, and it is travel from.
The directions suggest travel as somehow a recourse, as motivated.
Most of the poems from the middle of Bishop's career, from *A Cold
Spring* (1955) and from the book titled (like the poem) *Questions
of Travel* (1965), concentrate on some image or event that evokes
the distinctiveness of a particular place, whether a large place on a
familiarly, geographically mappable scale, like Key West or Brazil,
or some smaller place, like a filling station or a hospital for the insane
("Visits to St. Elizabeths"). Because such places seem strange and
yet remain familiar enough to fall within a public geography, they
preserve the idiosyncrasy of Bishop's early and unabashedly peculiar
poems, and yet set that peculiarity in an arena that other people
can more directly authenticate and share. The goal is not just to
choose and see those half-familiar places imaginatively; for after all,
as "Questions of Travel" says, in some sense they remain inevitably
"imagined places." Rather, the goal is to see them with a particular
kind of imagination that she can reach only by refracting her nar-
rowness through faraway imaginations, even though she must also

refract those others through her own. Instead of writing out of some private dream vision, then, as she does so often in *North & South*, she begins one poem ("Letter to N.Y.") by telling a friend that "In your next letter I wish you'd say / where you are going and what you are doing." Wish gives way to where. Hence the more mature Bishop seeks to imagine the public Brazil of geographers, rather than, putting it figuratively, the lonelier Brazil of the mind that erupted with a private strangeness in poems like "The Weed," "The Man-Moth," or "The Unbeliever."

"Questions of Travel" exposes an element of retreat in Bishop's movement from private to public, but her imagination of place is not always so apologetic. "At the Fishhouses," from *A Cold Spring*, ends with a forthright pronouncement completely opposite to the tentativeness in "Questions of Travel" and unlike anything in *North & South*. Its closing homage to the sea shows no sign of the cir-cumspection readers have come—perhaps rashly—to identify with Bishop:

> It is like what we imagine knowledge to be:
> dark, salt, clear, moving, utterly free,
> drawn from the cold hard mouth
> of the world, derived from the rocky breasts
> forever, flowing and drawn, and since
> our knowledge is historical, flowing, and flown.

This philosophical assertiveness and programmatic confidence does not seem the work of the same poet who wrote *North & South*. Something has changed.

It matters, though, that this confidence does not show until the end of, for Bishop, a rather long poem. First, she spends a lot of time earning her confidence, or trying to. The rhetorical strategy of "At the Fishhouses," with all its uncharacteristic bravado at the end, is inductive. It begins with details that slowly accumulate as if to build up to and justify the broad concluding assertions—to justify them rhetorically, though never with the close logic of argument. For the logic of syllogism Bishop substitutes the enticement of at-mosphere, of description that coaxes us to the strange from the perspective of one who knows it familiarly, yet is not entirely of it, who is both of the strange described world and of the ordinary world she describes it for.

> Although it is a cold evening,
> down by one of the fishhouses
> an old man sits netting,
> his net, in the gloaming almost invisible,
> a dark purple-brown,
> and his shuttle worn and polished.
> The air smells so strong of codfish
> it makes one's nose run and one's eyes water.

Immediately, the poem sets us into a deserted and distant place, and yet it sets us there as casually as if its world of seaside decay were our own world. It is not the world of many readers, and not even, any more, the world of the writer whose origin it evokes. The old man's world that fades into the metaphorical sunset (the gloaming) may come back the next morning, and for a few mornings after that, but its metaphorical morning is gone for ever. And yet the fading world comes across as if familiar, because words like "although" and "the" suggest *in medias res* that we already know about "the" fishhouses and about what fishermen do on cold evenings. The phrase "in the gloaming almost invisible" gives a sense, then, of something reduced to a latency that always has been and always will be. Though it refers to the net, it seems also to refer to the fisherman. Subject and object (fisherman and net) have both nearly evaporated into a nostalgic, twilight glow, leaving only activity itself. The activity they leave is the Fates' ancient metaphor, the transforming of time into culture, of the eternal into the temporal, whether by the fisherman's craft of tool building (net weaving) or, here, by the literary weaving of verbal art, the yet more fundamental medium and content of culture.

Such activity has gone on for a long time; the shuttle is "worn and polished." Bishop's presence will not change it, at least not for the fisherman or his world, which goes on, however fadingly, regardless of her. She feels immersed in his world, with its strong smell. *His* world affects *her*, making her "nose run and ... eyes water"; but she cannot affect it. She has changed from the earlier poems where she projects her imagined world out from herself and celebrates its imaginative power, as in "The Map," "The Imaginary Iceberg," "The Man-Moth," "The Weed," "The Unbeliever," and so on. Now, instead of projecting her mind onto the place, she tries, at least, to see the intransigent resistance of place, for it seems on

the verge of overflowing in an unrestrainable flood: "the heavy
surface of the sea, / swelling slowly as if considering spilling over."

Those words reverse the relation between land and sea that interested her in "The Map":

> Or does the land lean down to lift the sea from under,
> drawing it unperturbed around itself?
> Along the fine tan sandy shelf
> is the land tugging at the sea from under?
>
> .   .   .   .
>
> These peninsulas take the water between thumb and finger
> like women feeling for the smoothness of yard-goods.
>
> Mapped waters are more quiet than the land is,
> lending the land their waves' own conformation:
> and Norway's hare runs south in agitation,
> profiles investigate the sea, where land is.

In "The Map," the land reaches into the sea. The land is active—
it leans, lifts, draws, tugs, takes, feels, is less quiet, borrows what
the water lends, runs south, and investigates—whereas the sea is passive. But in "The Map," none of Bishop's words for the land—
land, sandy shelf, peninsulas, Norway's hare, profiles—and none of
her words for the sea refer to actual land or sea. They all refer
instead to the clay of cartographical imagination, to what a mapmaker, or, figuratively, a poet, can shape out of or project onto the
land and sea. From its title onward, "The Map" is not about actual
place but rather about a fanciful defiance of any standard in the
images we project onto place. Except, as Bishop's questioning reminds us ("Or does . . . ?"), those images never suggest a standard
until after we grant the exterior world an authority—as we ordinarily
and unthinkingly do—that it can never acquire inherently.

"At the Fishhouses" (1947) and the place-obsessed poems of Bishop's middle career grant or submit to the authority of external place.
They identify the issue as *where* we are: we are at the fishhouses.
A somewhat later poem, "Questions of Travel" (1957), concludes by
backing away from the turn to place only enough to reaffirm that
the only place we ever see is that we project from within. In "Questions of Travel" Bishop looks back nostalgically toward wish, but
with a jaded sound. Her opening words ("There are too many . . .")

complain of the old where, by contrast, an early poem like "The Map" or "The Imaginary Iceberg" sounds excited to discover the new. Even there, though, she continues the preoccupation with *where* that dominates "At the Fishhouses."

Who she is, she implies in "At the Fishhouses," has grown out of where she and her people have been. But the place where they have been is about to disappear, which will transform their sense of origin into a memory forever severed from the actual place remembered:

> The old man accepts a Lucky Strike.
> He was a friend of my grandfather.
> We talk of the decline in population
> and of codfish and herring
> while he waits for a herring boat to come in.
> There are sequins on his vest and on his thumb.
> He has scraped the scales, the principal beauty,
> from unnumbered fish with that black old knife,
> the blade of which is almost worn away.

Everything here appears on the edge of the end. The old fisherman is not a friend of Bishop's grandfather—he *was* a friend of him. That is gone now, the grandfather and the friendship with him, and the old fisherman seems about to follow. He acquiesces to the poet's distant manner of closeness, her friendly purchase of rapport. The bribe shows her distance from his world, even as his willingness to accept it shows her connection to it, an ambiguity that she presumably appreciates, setting her poem, as she does here and so often, on the edge where two worlds meet and overlap and never join. She gives him almost a parody of his profession—a lucky strike, as if to imply that is the only way he'll get any luck. In name, her little gift belongs to the sportfishing world of "The Fish," where she can toss back her prize and feel heroic for it. It has nothing to do with this fisherman's fishing. In his commercial, unheroic, blue-collar salt's world, he must wait for his fish, for his "boat to come in"; and in some sense the boat he now waits for most, looks to and expects the most, is the soon-to-come ferry of death, his and his world's. He is almost worn away, like his knife, like the population that declines, as if in mores as well as in numbers, so unlike the unnumbered fish, which are always the same.

The unchanging world of the fish, finally, intrigues Bishop more.
But she cannot turn to it easily. She spends half the poem working
up to it by describing the land, then the fisherman, then, in a
conspicuously transitional stanza, actually describing the ramp that
descends from land to sea, as if she needs to find some feature in
the physical landscape to draw her into the water, like a timid bather
stepping in slowly. Then at last, and with tones of self-conscious
profundity, she dives in:

> Cold dark deep and absolutely clear,
> element bearable to no mortal,
> to fish and to seals . . . One seal particularly
> I have seen here evening after evening.
> He was curious about me. He was interested in music;
> like me a believer in total immersion,
> so I used to sing him Baptist hymns.
>
> .   .   .   .
>
> Cold dark deep and absolutely clear,
> the clear gray icy water . . . Back, behind us,
> the dignified tall firs begin.

She introduces the water in an atmosphere of all-encompassing yet
unspecifiable mystery. Its depth suggests an ultimacy, almost a ubiquity; yet it is also distantly cold, too dark and clear to see. She so
romanticizes, on the one hand, the ocean's grandiose allure and, on
the other hand, its ominous invisibility that the combination of almost
opposed extremes implies that ordinary ocean has little to do with
what so attracts and intimidates her. Instead she puzzles over the
role that ordinary ocean can somehow figure in her own partly private
and partly representative array of fears and wishes.

The impulses to such figurings are vague but threatful, and hence
not easy to own up to. Every time Bishop gets a start at them, she
soon backs away. If the element she ruminates over is "bearable to
no mortal," then what draws her to it? Hence the glibly cliché
evasion, "to no mortal," lets her rationalize a further evasion. She
slides into an ellipsis and changes the subject to animal—that is, to
unambiguously mortal—comic relief, nervously relaxing with a little
satire of her immersion in place and her preoccupation with water.
Then she can move on. Moving on, therefore, means moving back
to the words she left off with, the words before her ellipsis that were

supposed to introduce her direct turn to the water, and that she left when she got fearful and distracted. But instead of returning to those words, she slides into yet another ellipsis, turning "Back, behind us" to the land of trees.

All this looping back adds up to a startling hesitation, as if both the length of her reluctance and the piling up of her repetitions measure the force of what she hesitates before. They evoke the sea's awesome breadth and uniformity; she can go back to it forever and always it will be "the same":

> I have seen it over and over, the same sea, the same,
> slightly, indifferently swinging above the stones,
> icily free above the stones,
> above the stones and then the world.

The land changes, the sea stays the same. Both evoke her past, one a fading past that soon she will recover only through memory, never through immediate sensation, and the other a past she can always recover. Strangely, because the sea's past never varies, it is somehow almost cosmically more capacious, and therefore less tangible than the past that escapes ubiquity to lodge in memory. That cosmic suggestiveness exacts from Bishop an awed humility, in which her repeated words and phrases ("the same," "above the stones") build an incantatory sound that culminates in the closing lines:

> If you tasted it, it would first taste bitter,
> then briny, then surely burn your tongue.
> It is like what we imagine knowledge to be:
> dark, salt, clear, moving, utterly free,
> drawn from the cold hard mouth
> of the world, derived from the rocky breasts
> forever, flowing and drawn, and since
> our knowledge is historical, flowing, and flown.

These lines define the difference between *wish* and *where*, a difference that shows in the way Bishop uses them, in effect, to revise the concluding vision of "The Man-Moth." The earlier poem ends with a melodramatic litany of *ifs* and a tasting of primeval waters, cool and pure. Here Bishop again closes with a sagacious-sounding *if* and a tasting of primeval waters. But this time the waters appear on an oceanic rather than a quaintly miniature scale, and

they taste—or would taste—bitter. The change signals a movement
from the nervous thrill of fantastic, individual wish to the settled
disillusion of ordinary, public place. The public knowledge celebrated
in the final line is historical, received, in contrast to the asserted,
original knowledge of "The Map," in which the printer's excitement
reveals emotion that "exceeds its cause," tempting Bishop to think
that the "countries pick their colors." The wished-for open sesame
of imagination in early poems like "The Map" and "The Man-Moth"
thus gives way to a resigned-to satisfaction at natural specificity in
the poems of Bishop's mid-career. In "At the Fishhouses," the final,
cadenced hush before "it," before the ocean, betrays how desperately
in the first part of the poem Bishop strives to keep the evanescent
place from slipping away before she can trap it in poetic capture.
She apparently hopes to arrest its elusiveness simply by surrendering
to her grandfather's and her childhood's world at its last tide of
fullness.

If in the first part of the poem Bishop tries not to lose, then in
the last part she tries to recover what is inevitably lost. As "The Sea
& Its Shore" is her "As I Ebb'd with the Ocean of Life," so "At the
Fishhouses" is, more loosely, her "Out of the Cradle Endlessly Rock-
ing." For the "it" that she describes takes on a resonance that works
for her like a subtler version of the seaside aria that releases Whitman's solitary song. He feels the bird's inspiration, but somehow
loses it again until he muses back over his past and recognizes how
his song is bound intimately to an enabling vision of tragic loss, to
the ancient muse of memory that inspires, that gives, by taking away.
For Bishop, "it," as she obscurely pronominalizes her material here,
is not a bird's song. It is the ocean, our evolutionary origin, suggestive
also of our amniotic origins in our mothers (the cradle out of which
we endlessly rock). Yet she stretches "it" out syntactically so that it
starts to refer to knowledge as well as to the ocean.[3] That blurring
of reference is no coincidence, for knowledge is the earliest reach
back of memory, and the first reach forward of ambition, and therefore, mythologically, biblically (the tree of knowledge), and psycho-
logically, the beginning of the guilt through which memory breeds
imagination. If Whitman displaces his anxiety over origins onto a
pair of birds, as if foisting on them some traumatic but comfortingly
distant displacement of the primal scene, then Bishop (coming after

Darwin, whom she admired[4]), a little more evasive, sees a more generalized ultimacy of origins in the oceanic waters, in something evolutionarily still more primeval. As Whitman pursues the recovery of his private origin, Bishop pursues the recovery of her public origin.

But it is unrecoverable. It is too "dark," which makes it invisible, and yet too "clear," which also makes it invisible, too fluidly "moving, utterly free." What it is, therefore, she cannot or at least does not say. Instead, she says "It is *like* what we *imagine*," and then turns to metaphor. Unable to recover the thing itself, she tries to recover its thrice-removed shadow, removed once by metaphor, and again by metaphorizing not "it" so much as what we *imagine* that, at the third remove, it derives *from*. Moreover, she tropes what it comes from in a way that reveals how reluctant we are and, as Derrida might insist, how impossible it is to imagine the independent mystery of our origins. We cannot help projecting onto the ancient past some feature from our present. Here Bishop sees in the past the bodily fears that provoke the very anxiousness that makes us wonder about origins in the first place. That is, she tropes what "it" comes from as what it leads to: the human. She invokes its central features as a mouth and breasts. Still, she complicates that bodily metaphor by pairing it with uncorporeal adjectives that figure its cold inaccessibility. Its mouth is cold and hard, its breasts, even more forbidding, are rocky. The mixed metaphors expose a mixed attraction and resistance to thinking of such elemental sources as human. For if they are human then we might bear more responsibility for them or more relation to them. She thus has a stake in failing to recover the primeval mystery that nevertheless fascinates her.

Hence even as she resorts, in part, to a more or less accessibly human metaphor, she evasively generalizes it in a way that obscures a yet more latent metaphor of the human. That earlier metaphor, suggested just enough for us to glimpse its repression, is of birth. She represses it by confining its expression to features that are not exclusively maternal—a mouth and breasts. But the repression shines through that pretense of generic reference because we associate the feminine and maternal with the idea of coming from something or someone who has breasts and a mouth. The carefully generalized anatomy and the reifying adjectives—cold, hard, and rocky—make the maternal seem irksome and defended against. Such adjectives betray a comfort in projecting onto our origins a forbidding discomfort. If the maternal is so harsh, then perhaps Bishop need feel less burden for the harshness of her own relation to her mother, or the fantasy of some harshness in her not being a mother herself. Her feelings here are as mixed as her metaphors. She metaphorizes maternal origin as something severe, and yet rests in awe of it as something that repeats itself in us but that in some sense we can never fully repeat.

All these complications and their aggrandizingly portentous phrasing lead some readers to dismiss the end of "At the Fishhouses," not implausibly and yet not quite satisfactorily, as a posturing for profundity.[5] Such a response underestimates how thoughtfully the earlier, concrete parts of the poem lay the ground for the more reflective seascape to follow, where Bishop thinks about the water, and, in a sense, sees herself, even if she protectively metaphorizes herself as her origins. As the land calls up the specific associations of her recognizable past, so the water calls up the vaguer associations of a past intensely felt but nevertheless unrecognizable because it is "forever . . . , flowing, and flown." The small things of a familiar place, the wheelbarrows, lobster pots, fish tubs, and herring scales, contain the hard specifiable knowledge she can hold in mind and hand. But the largest things, in their ungraspably oceanic scale, she can never confidently specify and identify. Bishop thus uses the change in the poem both to suggest the specially ruminative aura of the ocean— "meditation and water are wedded forever," as Melville's Ishmael says—and to suggest the allure she feels in that reflectiveness. She likes to reflect, perhaps partly because she finds it difficult to know or understand what she sees when (in the other sense of the word *reflection*) her meditation reflects back on herself. "At the Fishhouses" is thus an intimately self-conscious poem, cautiously feeling out the relation between place and identity, and dissolving, finally, in the watery mystery of its own contemplation.

On its grand scale, then, "At the Fishhouses" does things much like some other poems from the middle of Bishop's career, where she works on a smaller scale geographically but explores just as keenly the relation between identity and place, whether someone else's place, as in "Filling Station," or a public place that corrupts the private, as in "Varick Street," or, as in "Insomnia," a thoroughly and even troublingly private place. In "Insomnia," Bishop embeds the farsighted gaze from the end of "At the Fishhouses" within a claustrophobic reflectiveness from which she nearsightedly envies the embedded farsight. If that seems confusing, it is; to tell about it she needs parentheses that themselves embed both an "and perhaps" and a "but," and then quickly give way to another "or" and a "perhaps," all in a short first stanza of only six trimeter lines and one sentence:

> The moon in the bureau mirror
> looks out a million miles
> (and perhaps with pride, at herself,
> but she never, never smiles)
> far and away beyond sleep, or
> perhaps she's a daytime sleeper.

In this oppressively unmythological context, it sounds a little strange to call the moon "she" instead of "it." Usually, by contrast, when people look in a "bureau mirror" they see what they put the mirror there to reflect: themselves. Thus the moon, as yet distinctive mainly for its unsmiling sorrow, begins by sounding like some enviably proud projection of herself and her own sadness.

But the next lines reverse that cautious identifying with the moon: "By the universe deserted, / *she*'d tell it to go to hell." Abruptly, the italics distinguish the moon from Bishop, or from the poem's speaker, as if to say that the moon's willingness to tell the universe off looks extraordinary because it diverges so far from Bishop's temptation to see the moon as ordinary, as maybe more farsighted but otherwise like herself. If the moon is sad, then, its sadness brings out that she herself is sadder. For Bishop lacks the pride to defend herself, which brings into sharper focus the first stanza's implication that she cannot even see herself. She looks into the mirror and instead of seeing herself she sees the moon. And even that secondary, mirrored moon, in turn, as if to complete the taunt of its superiority, does what Bishop cannot do. It looks out pridefully at itself.

Of course, though, it does no such thing. The very feebleness of Bishop's conceit brings out the stake she must have in it to bother drawing it out with such strained cleverness. It serves some purpose for which she is willing to undergo trial by her own indulgently self-pitying wit. She feels a gain in imagining a moon she can envy, because her pride has so collapsed that she cannot express it in relation simply to herself. Instead, she invents a comparison to belittle

herself. Indeed, she knows the conceit is feeble, because the ac-
knowledgment of hopelessness and the relegation of hope to mere
conceit become the point.[6] She must "wrap up care," she concludes,
"in a cobweb," as if to say that she must sweep it away with the
other hopes that she now realizes can never do more than gather
dust like the rubbish she now sees them as, and throw it away. But,
as she tells it, she doesn't exactly trash her hope. Instead, she consigns
it, or, more tentatively, tells herself to consign it to the enfeebled
world of her conceit, tells herself to

> drop it down the well
>
> into that world inverted
> where left is always right,
> where the shadows are really the body,
> where we stay awake all night,
> where the heavens are shallow as the sea
> is now deep, and you love me.

Those last words hit with a small shock on a first reading. They
force us to see "Insomnia" as a love poem, or a poem of failed love,
and so to reread and notice afresh the resort to secondariness, to
reflection and shadow and inversion. The poem begins so narcis-
sistically self-absorbed that at the end the word "we," and even more,
the words "you" and "love" come as surprises. Bishop hoards them
till last and gives them the extra force of rhyme (as Dickinson often
does). The halt of conclusion makes the sudden rhyme more no-
ticeable, an effect she further enhances by closing with the poem's
only couplet, which further underlines the rhyme and its suddenness.
Her lover, then, loves her only in the backwards world, which is to
say, her lover doesn't love her. Their bodies go through merely the
incorporeal motions of "shadows." The moon, if deserted, would tell
its lover to go to hell—meaning that Bishop, deserted, unloved,
would like to tell hers to do the same, but cannot.[7]

Only in the mirror's "world inverted" can she receive the love
she gives, splitting her own world like "The Gentleman of Shalott."
But the split cuts out herself, the source of her love in the first place,
for the mirror reflects the moon not with but rather instead of herself.
The secondary moon reflected in the mirror looks back at its primary
form. It thus sees itself (or so Bishop chooses to imagine) in relation
to an original will, whereas Bishop does not see even her reflected,
secondary self. Things are bad enough so that she would like to

salvage even that merely reflected self, would like to see herself derivatively in relation to her lover. But she cannot do even that, since her lover doesn't care. Which explains why Bishop herself, or the persona she chooses in this poem, is less than secondary, that is, cannot see even her reflection. She has no belief in her own self, her ego. She still wants to wish, but no longer believes in it enough to bother.

As in "The Man-Moth," the moon figures as the object and emblem of aspiration. In some respects, "Insomnia" is a poem of wish like Bishop's early poems. She wishes to sustain the mirror world's illusion of love, recalling her celebrations of illusion as imagination in poems like "The Map," "The Imaginary Iceberg," and "The Unbeliever." But "The Unbeliever" discriminates among illusions, preferring its title character's anxious fantasy to the cloud's and the gull's mirages of complacency. Here in "Insomnia" Bishop is fully as anxious as the unbeliever, but stays awake amidst the sort of fear that drives him to sleep. The unbeliever falls asleep to dream the vision that Bishop celebrates him for. But in "Insomnia" something has changed, for the dream she clings to is yet more fragile than the precarious unbeliever's; it is a waking dream, a deliberate vision that will disappear if she submits to the unpredictable, weedy vagaries of sleeping dreams ("The Unbeliever," "The Weed," "Sleeping Standing Up"). In other words, Bishop sometimes holds onto wish in these poems from the middle of her career, but she finds that wish has been compromised. Her earlier celebrations seem innocent by comparison. She wishes for her lover's love, but that does not bring it to her. Wish does not work. The only way she can bring herself that love is to stack the deck by controlling the circumstances of wish, that is, by controlling *where*. Hence she stays awake, so she can sustain the where of waking imagination, as she pleads in the frantically reiterated "where" that begins all four lines before the ironic last line that defines what makes that where so insisted on, namely, that it is the only place she can win the love she longs for. She thus reverses her plea to the "Roosters":

> what right have you to . . .
>
> cry "Here!" and "Here!"
> and wake us here where are
> unwanted love, conceit and war?

In "Roosters" she does not want the wakeful world's love. She would rather sleep where she can dream of wanted love. And in "Roosters," with its fury of implied resentment at male heterosexual aggression, both between men and by men against women, she vaguely, by little more than a process of elimination, implies her preference for a gentler, presumably lesbian love that she associates with sleep. That implication by mere default hardly sounds optimistic, except by comparison with "Insomnia," where the gentle bed of hope has become a bed of disillusion. Even in that grim early poem, "The Weed," with its own bed of disillusion, the speaker or poet seems condemned not only to disillusion but also to an ever-rejuvenating imagination. However frightfully that imagination sprouts up with a will of its own, its liveliness still carries an odd reassurance. Sleep brings dream, a mixed blessing, but a blessing nevertheless, like the anxious triumph of imagination and poetry that dream represents. Thus dream, in *North & South*, takes us to the geography of wish, most readily figured in that outer landscape, the moon, whether for the Man-Moth or for the baby of "Songs for a Colored Singer," III:

> Lullaby.
> Sleep on and on,
> war's over soon.
> Drop the silly, harmless toy,
> pick up the moon.

In "Insomnia," though, sleep is no longer the land of hope, for hope seems less a feature of mind, whether sleeping or waking, than, more feebly, a feature of place, as it tends to be throughout *A Cold Spring* and *Questions of Travel*. To be sure, the power of place is at its most precarious in "Insomnia," but that seems to be why Bishop pleads for it so urgently in her litany of "where," "where," "where," and "where." She troubles to define her hopeless remnant of hope in terms of place rather than, as in the earlier poems, in some authentic terms of hope itself. Even the mid-career poems that we might think of as more hopeful express those feelings through a preoccupation with place, as in "Filling Station," "Twelfth Morning; or What You Will," or "Song for the Rainy Season," which takes much of the same imagery Bishop used more fitfully in "The Weed" and tames it, domesticates it, locates it in a specific, geographical place rather than letting it float in a threateningly vague topography of mind. More and more, place becomes a preoccupation for her, though the places themselves vary in scale from, most frequently, the domestic, middle sizes of houses or of particular vistas or landscapes, to, at opposite extremes, the imprisoning claustrophobia of "Insomnia" on the one hand and, on the other, the unenclosable, continental vastness that she treats so variously in "Questions of Travel," or the ominous "Arrival at Santos," or the grandly historical "Brazil, January 1, 1502."

On January 1, 1502, the first Portuguese sailed into Guanabara Bay, which they mistook for the mouth of a great river. Hence the name Rio de Janeiro, and the beginning of Bishop's poem:

> Januaries, Nature greets our eyes
> exactly as she must have greeted theirs:
> every square inch filling in with foliage—
> big leaves, little leaves, and giant leaves,
> blue, blue-green, and olive,
> with occasional lighter veins and edges,
>
>   .   .   .   .   .
>
> up in the air—up, rather, in the leaves—
> purple, yellow, two yellows, pink,
> rust red and greenish white;
> solid but airy.

With no particular extravagance, Bishop remarkably makes description an act of thoughtful intelligence by the way she repeatedly sees one thing in relation to another. She sees our vision in relation to the early explorers' vision. The big leaves take definition from the little leaves, and then even from the giant leaves, reversing the sequence, as when she says "a year, a minute, an hour" in "The Weed." She connects blue, as if it can't properly be seen by itself, to its cousin blue-green, and blue-green then to *its* cousin on the other side, olive. And then all three colors she relates to "occasional lighter veins and edges"; then she links yellows and reds to other shades of the same hues, and sees their solidity as somehow linked to their airiness, its opposite. As so often, in her determined empiricism she preserves the trail of her changing mind.[8] Her rejected thought that the flowers float in the air stays unerased apparently because it can still render how loosely they cling to their leaves. Thus even the thought she discards tells something she needs, both to describe and to show how the description impinges on mind. Because her subject is not in itself the land as it looked before the Portuguese came. If it were, she could have told about December 31, 1501, about the *end* of something. Nor is her subject only the landscape. It is also the perception of that landscape, and how that perception begot something called Brazil.

For the empirical vision of landscape gives way to a vision that projects the human imagination onto what it sees, calling attention to the poem's epigraph from Kenneth Clark's *Landscape into Art:* not nature or landscape, but "embroidered nature . . . tapestried landscape," sounding much more aggressive than the epigraph might suggest. When the poem moves from flora to fauna, suddenly its projections grow more conspicuously ideological than any particular form, such as tapestry or embroidery, would require. Bishop refers to the "big symbolic birds," and insists that

> Still in the foreground there is Sin:
> five sooty dragons near some massy rocks.
> The rocks are . . .
> threatened from underneath by moss
> in lovely hell-green flames,
> attacked above
> by scaling-ladder vines, oblique and neat.

Presumably, Bishop expects us, as heirs of a realist tradition and readers of Robert Frost, to recognize that those birds cannot be *inherently* symbolic. Rather, they are *seen* symbolically, and seen that way not by whoever looks, but instead by those who look from a particular perspective, namely, the Portuguese explorers of the title and first two lines: "Januaries, Nature greets our eyes / exactly as she must have greeted theirs." Nature has stayed the same (at least in part of Brazil, surely not in Rio). But "our eyes" have changed, or can change.

The Portuguese explorers, heirs of a medieval intellectual tradition that, like their "dream of wealth and luxury," is "already out of style when they left home," see nature allegorically and symbolically, as Nature. They see lizards not simply as lizards. Instead, they see them as background to an ideology that they project onto the lizards, and seen through which the ordinary reptiles shed the skin a naturalist might see and don instead a symbolist's dragon suit of Sin. The chapter of Kenneth Clark's book that Bishop quotes describes the transformation from a medieval world view of Symbolism to a renaissance and modern view of Realism or empiricism that allows us to see nature as landscape.[9] Bishop slides into the symbolizing vision without any attribution. She leaves us to *deduce* that the description is oddly perspectivized, and to deduce through whom, and thus to alert ourselves to an allegorizing vision that casts the world into alternate camps: on one side, the devil's dragons of heathendom, and on the other side, presumably, the angels' battalions of those she soon names more tellingly as "the Christians."

At first, the consequences of such allegorizing show with no more than insidious subtlety. Once the animals are allegorized, then the plants that at first Bishop describes so neutrally, by size and color, act like willful agents. They 'threaten' and 'attack.' And the idea that they attack with scaling ladders, metaphorically the equipment of Europeans, indirectly attributes the vision of attack to the metaphorizing Portuguese rather than to the unthinking "vines, oblique and neat."

All these tricks with plants and animals reveal how the explorers see the New World through their Old World ideology of size and sex, culminating in the last five lines:

> they ripped away into the hanging fabric,
> each out to catch an Indian for himself—
> those maddening little women who kept calling,
> calling to each other (or had the birds waked up?)
> and retreating, always retreating, behind it.

Had the poem begun with such language it would have been hardly intelligible. Why are the women little? What is *it*, given that, much more vastly than any two-dimensional fabric, *it* takes on some vast and seemingly ever-recedable depth? Looking back, hindsight can unveil what had been developing in the poem so gradually that, probably even before we quite realized, it prepared us to apprehend the rape of both the women and the landscape that the poem ends with.[10] *It* becomes, retrospectively, the landscape of stanza one and the epigraph that had at first seemed neutral or even benignly hospitable, as it "greets our eyes." But our eyes, apparently, do funny things in return, things we only gradually discover as the poem unfolds, and that, once we recognize them, we can see working earlier and earlier in the poem, embroidering nature, tapestrying landscape. Thus the ferns, more suggestively than we probably realized at first, are no longer simply "big" or "little" or even "giant" like the leaves but become—or are seen as—"monster ferns," a phrase that retrospectively sounds the more ominous for having a line all to itself. Going back further, and still wondering over the peculiar imposition of some uniform category—smallness—on the Indian women, we can see with the self-consciousness of hindsight that right from the beginning Bishop has feminized nature: "Nature greets our eyes   exactly as she must have greeted theirs." So far as I know, this is the only poem where Bishop subscribes to that familiar metaphor of a female Nature, a metaphor so commonplace that it usually goes unrecognized and taken for granted as natural fact.

But it is not natural fact. To see nature as feminine is to objectify (to make an object of) femininity, which in the heterosexual world of this particular poem makes the subject—grammatically the perceiver of and actor upon Nature—masculine.[11] Men do, women are done to. Right away, then, Bishop speaks in a conspiring language of male aggression and female exclusion, the more insidious because the guise of Nature veils the distortion as innocently natural truth, when, on the contrary, this is probably her most intricately perspectivized poem and among her most ironic.[12] She begins by speaking in the voice that the poem will rebel against, as if to suggest that such language is so pervasive that even she who will criticize it cannot help being infected by it. As in one of Browning's dramatic monologues, then, her language gradually reveals its own mask, eventually letting just enough irony slip through to achieve a ventriloquist's satirical distance:

> The lizards scarcely breathe; all eyes
> are on the smaller, female one, back-to,
> her wicked tail straight up and over,
> red as a red-hot wire.

The account of animal lust, all but specified as male lust poised for

violence, and for the violence of many against one, implies a vicious human analogue: these male explorers are lizards. They are themselves the dragonlike Sin they project onto the New World's landscape, as Bishop quickly goes on to confirm: "Just so the Christians."
Then something startling happens:

> Just so the Christians, hard as nails,
> tiny as nails, and glinting,
> in creaking armor, came and found it all,
> not unfamiliar:

Suddenly, the Christians are tiny. In itself that may not seem remarkable, but once we look back from the ending, where the Indian women appear as "little," and where the whole poem's violence fits the explosively rabid lizard scene to suggest a male European fantasy of inherent magnitude and right, then the notion that the Europeans are tiny seems all askew. Indeed, for a moment, Bishop has abruptly reversed perspective, so that instead of seeing through European eyes she now sees how treacherously the Europeans appear insignificant against the dwarfing immensity of Brazilian forest. They especially look tiny from the perspective of the Indians, who see the invaders, at first, from a distance both geographically (as they sail forward from the horizon) and culturally. That distance tragically allows the Indians to underestimate the Europeans, even as the Europeans tragically underestimate the Indians. By reversing perspective even so briefly, Bishop puts the European delusions in her own unsentimental perspective. They misperceive the Indians not simply because they are nasty men or nasty Europeans and cannot see Indian innocence, but more because that is the way of cultural collision. Everyone misperceives everyone else.
They see wrongly because they cannot see anew. Instead of seeing something astonishingly strange in the New World, they find it "not unfamiliar: / . . . corresponding . . . / to an old dream of wealth and luxury." They approach even the Indians, then, as commodity—wealth—rather than as culture.[13] Bishop says they take the Indian women as a "brand-new pleasure," but as she describes it they seem to see the Indians no more authentically, no more newly, than they see the landscape. Though the pleasure may be new in the sense of its easy availability, they respond to it in an old way. For they see

the Indians as slaves and concubines ready for the picking, and in that sense they assimilate the Indians to the roles that darker people, African blacks and Moors, already played in Portugal.

Yet even as they impose their Portuguese precedents on the new land, they both find and create something distinctively different from anything they already know. They breed a new people and a new culture; this poem is very much about the birth of culturally and racially hybrid Brazil. Historically, the poem seems a hybrid itself, as Bishop relies on no particular historical account but rather chooses and mixes what can best represent Brazil's colonial fate. The actual voyage that touched at the present site of Rio de Janeiro in January, 1502, was the second voyage of Amerigo Vespucci, but Bishop takes nothing in particular from Vespucci's account, which does not fit her poem's purposes.[14] Rather, she seems to use several other famous early accounts, materials she refers to in her Time-Life book on Brazil written at about the same time as the poem.[15] In the book she quotes Pero Vaz de Caminha, scribe for the first Portuguese to land in Brazil (1500), noting that he took special interest in the Indian women. "In Brazil," she says, "it was only natural for them [the Portuguese] to become eager miscegenationists almost immediately." There she also refers to Samuel Putnam's history of Brazilian literature. Its first chapter, called "Landscape Is Not All," begins with Caminha and then quotes the famous sixteenth-century Jesuits (whom Bishop calls "fascinating" in *Brazil*) Fathers José de Anchieta and Manuel da Nobrega, who both compare the Brazilian forests to Portuguese gardens, as Bishop's poem does. Anchieta dwells especially on the "beautiful birds" (so does Vespucci), which become the "big symbolic birds" in the poem. In *Brazil*, Bishop says—with a characteristic air of bemusement—that the first map of Brazil (1502) sketches in the trees "lined up formally as in a Portuguese garden, and under them sits a group of giant macaws, presumably to give explorers some idea of what to expect." Nobrega's words seem especially suggestive of Bishop's poem. "The woods," he says, "resemble huge gardens and orchards, and I do not recall having seen any arras cloth that was as beautiful."[16]

The explorers thus confront a world different from their own, but see it as if it were their own. They allegorize the landscape as a work of art, an arras or tapestry "fresh as if just finished / and taken off the frame." They treat nature as we—at our most credulous—

treat art, as an interpretable code, as allegorizable: Lizards represent Sin. But when Bishop transforms perspective and scale so that the *explorers* become the lizards, then their allegory turns around and snares them in their own trap. To allegorize, then, is to become allegorized. In Bishop's natural, unbeliever's wisdom, to see animals as Sin by your own creed is in itself to sin against the common creed of nature. Since the New World that they mistake for their own world extended is not, after all, their own world, it changes them (at least eventually, over the generations) as much as they change it.

Bishop's own allegorizing, her turning of the lizards into her own morality play, floats free of the explorers' self-deception because she does it ironically — to satirize their doing it in earnest. Thus by the end, when they rip into the fabric, the poem has thoroughly distanced its own perspective from the perspective of the language it still intermittently ventriloquizes. When Bishop says that the explorers "ripped away into the hanging fabric," the verb, with its double connotation of raping both the women and the landscape, is all in her own voice. But when she calls the women "those maddening little women" she allows us to hear how the violent verb in her own appalled voice gives way to a befuddled patronizing as her language slides back into the explorers' perspective. She seems to have chosen the word "women" with full deliberateness, for the first surviving draft says "little Indians" rather than "little women."[17] Of course, these women are not little in any objective sense. Their perceived littleness shows the invaders' frustration at their incapacity to grasp the women, both culturally and physically, a frustration especially audible in the slangy condescension of words like "those," which consigns all the women to one category; "maddening," which blames all the conflicts on the women's unreasonable stubbornness; and "little women," which echoes that timeworn phrase of masculine reassurance, "the little woman." The women here become prey, uncertainly distinguishable from the beautiful birds that the explorers admire as pets but no doubt find hard to catch.

But unlike the pretty macaws, the women keep calling "to each other." They talk, which disorients the explorers by its party-spoiling implication that the women are people of will like themselves rather than dumb animals of prey. Bishop's phrasing here reveals that she also had in mind another encounter between "explorer" and "little woman," for she repeats the ideology and the actual words of "The

Smallest Woman in the World," by the Brazilian Clarice Lispector. In Bishop's translation, Lispector's story (freely excerpted) begins this way: "The French explorer, Marcel Pretre, hunter and man of the world, came across . . . the smallest of the smallest pygmies in the world. . . . Feeling an immediate necessity for order and for giving names to what exists, he called her Little Flower. And in order to be able to classify her among the recognizable realities, he immediately began to collect facts about her. . . . [Her] tiny race, retreating, always retreating, has finished hiding away in the heart of Africa."[18]

This beginning to Lispector's story (which later gets more complicated) matches "Brazil, January 1, 1502" in ways that highlight certain issues in the poem. In each text, explorer, by custom male ("man of the world"), confronts "native," uncoincidentally female. It is uncoincidental because both Lispector and Bishop intensify the explorer's vision of native as object by overlaying it with his vision of woman as object. Still, the use of gender to intensify colonial trespass suggests not that gender conflict is secondary, but rather that, as a discord of both Old World and New, the conflict between genders is even more constant than the conflict between explorers and explored. What the invaders do to women makes a metaphor for what they do to landscape and culture, which indicates that what they do to the New World is in some respects a product of what they do to women and, more basically, of the cultural and psychological weaknesses that impel them to abuse women.

The explorer figure feels at once fascinated and mystified by feminine smallness. It encourages his sense of woman as object — Lispector even uses the word "toy" — but also gives her a "maddening" distinctiveness that frustrates his defensive wish to assimilate her to the familiar, "to classify her among the recognizable realities," whether of Linnaeus or of patrician Portugal. He thus tries to claim power by naming: Little Flower, Rio de Janeiro. He could have asked the name, but he does not acknowledge the "natives' " authority to name what had been their own land or even their own selves. The act of naming either another adult or what at least had been other adults' land is an act of appropriation. And in each case the particular names they choose redouble the appropriation by defining the named in relation to the namer: *Little* in relation to the man who sees his own size as norm, and *January* because the explorers' arrival in a time the explorers call January supposedly inaugurates all that can matter for the named place.

And the tragedy, Bishop suggests by her title, is that by creating a new place—Brazil—the explorers' arrival does indeed inaugurate what will most matter, for the change they bring to New World culture redefines it as Brazil. That change and its tragic circumstances fit both Bishop's anxiety over creativity and her mid-career preoccupation with place. She describes the creation of Brazil in violence and rape, and yet also pays homage to the cultural and bodily trauma of its birth, because that trauma begets the identity and heritage of the place she loves. Even if the memorializing of ancestry smacks of romanticizing, Bishop goes ahead with it presumably because "since / our knowledge is historical," as she says at the end of "At the Fishhouses," Brazil's past will be memorialized and hence romanticized one way or the other, so it had better be done with her sharp focus on the particular, unromantic details of conflict that the explorers themselves cannot see or understand, because they see only what they already know.

As the New World resists their recognition and understanding, so it also resists their physical appropriation, even as women can never be effaced by men. Bishop uses the exact same phrase in translation and poem. The indigenous worlds of the "little women" and of Little Flower keep "retreating, always retreating" behind *it*, behind landscape, the ultimate mask. The explorers rip into Nature as if it were art, which they can destroy, and do. But the difference between Nature and art is that one is the putty of human imagination and the other is not. Nature can be ripped apart, but it cannot be appropriated. Something about it will always retreat to where it can stay the same. After four and a half centuries, "Nature greets our eyes / exactly as she must have greeted theirs."

In "The Armadillo," another poem from the "Brazil" section of *Questions of Travel*, Bishop again takes up how a kind of cultural greed ravages both our landscape and ourselves. When she begins "Brazil, January 1, 1502" by likening our own vision to that of the Portuguese whom, at that point in the poem, we cannot yet know she will describe as marauding ravagers, she gives her lyrical rhapsodizing a treacherous seductiveness. For though it begins the poem with what, by the end, seems a startling suggestion—the idea that something essential has stayed unviolated for four and a half centuries—nevertheless, by the end she suggests also that what has remained the same is not so much the landscape itself as our perception of its otherness. That is what so frustrates the explorers, who resist acknowledging what they do not understand, and so defend against it. The perception of otherness, therefore, encompasses not only the appreciation of Nature's beauty but also the objectifying of its beauty into some fantasy of ready fodder for sexual and economic appetite.

In "The Armadillo," appetite at first seems much more innocent, for at first the greed seems to be only for the beautiful spectacle of fire balloons at night. But that is a dangerous beauty, legally forbidden, and "against the sky," Bishop says, "hard / to tell" from Venus or Mars, traditional figures of a more covetous appetite like that of the Portuguese explorers. The treacherous fire balloons evoke the ruin people risk ravaging on themselves and the place they love—the place Bishop warily celebrates—for the transient gain of one night's beauty. The balloons float up high "between / the kite sticks of the Southern Cross," the traditional symbol of Brazil,[19] but Brazil's beauty dangerously camouflages its tragedies. And so Bishop's images fall with the relentless logic of the fire balloons crashing to gravity. She says that it is hard to tell the balloons from Venus, just as their "light / . . . comes and goes, like hearts"; from Mars, just as they recall the Allies' fire bombing of Germany in World War II, which drove Robert Lowell—to whom she dedicates the poem—to refuse military service and go to jail; and more subtly, from "the pale green one," the moon, just as their self-destructive beauty hints at Lowell's chronic lunacy, which Bishop knew too well.[20]

Suddenly, at the end, Bishop forsakes tonal consistency and the relentless web of subtle images and all at once shifts to sweeping phrases, pleading italics, and urgent exclamation marks:

> *Too pretty, dreamlike mimicry!*
> *O falling fire and piercing cry*
> *and panic, and a weak mailed fist*
> *clenched ignorant against the sky!*

With her sudden tragic oracularity, vocative "O" and all, Bishop gives up the measured caution of her ordinary poetic manner. Reasonable protest has made no impression. The balloons are already illegal, but that has not mattered. Bishop feels, in effect, that she has to break the rules of discreet discourse to get across the tragedy of breaking more fundamental rules. But she shows no hope that her plea will change anyone's actions, will keep anyone from launching fire balloons—or love, bombs, or madness. Fire balloons, and the love, war, and madness that they figure, are "too pretty," too alluring in their immediate promise for us to do more than shake a hopeless fist at them. That fist closes the poem in heroicized frustration. The "ignorant" armadillo cannot know its own role as vehicle for Bishop's defiance, but by displacing her anger onto the dumb animal she also manages to make her outrage look more absolute, more instinctive. Her defiance may be futile, but her resort to anthropomorphism gives its futility poignance, as does the sorry inevitability that even that impotent "fist" relies on the violence that calls forth its protest.

Nevertheless, that futility, however poignant, combined with what Richard Wilbur has called the sudden impatience of the changed tone,[21] exposes a wide chasm between tenor and vehicle, between the vehemence of Bishop's protest and the modesty of what provokes it, a gap that actually opens earlier in the poem. Fire balloons, after all, are not fire bombs, and the burning of an owls' nest, scaring of an armadillo, and singeing of a rabbit torment us less than the fire bombing of Dresden. Such damage would not stop the devotees of fire balloons. At the same time, the distance between tenor and vehicle is what Bishop complains about, namely, the balloons' beauty— "*too pretty*"—disguises their danger. Beauty itself, then, is dangerous, potentially treacherous.

All this Bishop casts at Lowell, as if to suggest some explosive danger in *his* beauty, some chasm between his own perception of beauty's lure and its treachery. Much as her poem lauds his courage in refusing to join a war even more fouled than wars need be, it also laments his madness and implies some link between his madness and his imagination, as if to say of his poetry: it's not worth it. She feels an anxiousness over the cost of imagination that she suggests others should feel as well, especially Lowell. Indeed, outside the poem she later praised and excoriated him on just that point. Poetry, she thought, came easily for him, when it was a struggle for her. Even some of his finest poetry, she insisted, he should never publish because it would hurt the people his poems refer to.[22]

Lowell responded in print, both in prose and in poetry. For surely Lowell's blurb for the book jacket of Bishop's 1969 *Complete Poems* not only praises her but also, whether Lowell realized it or not, acknowledges and reacts painfully to "The Armadillo": "I am sure no living poet is as curious and observant as Miss Bishop. What cuts so deeply is that each poem is inspired by her own tone, a tone of large, grave tenderness and sorrowing amusement. She is too sure of herself for empty mastery and breezy plagiarism, too interested for confession and musical monotony, too powerful for mismanaged fire, and too civilized for idiosyncratic incoherence."[23] It is a startling statement. Lowell, still hurt by Bishop's poem, praises her observant ability to cut deeply, to manage the wayward "fire" that her poem blames him for failing to manage. Then he launches into an astonishing litany of praise, astonishing because, in the tradition of backhanded praise for the restrained "Miss Bishop," he praises her especially for what she does *not* do. Moreover, the things she does not do amount to a complete catalogue of everything Lowell's critics blame *him* for doing, so that in effect he damns her for not doing anything so grand except, ironically, the grandest things he failed to do himself.[24] Here, as so often in his poems, Lowell sounds wounded but surprises us with his self-critical honesty.

In "Skunk Hour," Lowell's poetic response and one of his finest and most famous poems, he is no less surprisingly self-critical or honest, but a good deal more defensive.[25] "The dedication," he later wrote, "is to Elizabeth Bishop, because re-reading her suggested a way of breaking through the shell of my old manner. Her rhythms, idiom, images, and stanza structure seemed to belong to a later century. 'Skunk Hour' is modeled on Miss Bishop's 'The Armadillo,' a much better poem and one I had heard her read and had later carried around with me. Both 'Skunk Hour' and 'The Armadillo' use short line stanzas, start with drifting description and end with a single animal."[26] He might have noted other similarities as well, for his poem leaves a trail of footprints back to hers. "This is the time of year," Bishop begins; "The season's ill—" Lowell echoes. Bishop's "Climbing the mountain height," becomes Lowell's "climbed the hill's skull"; her "light / that comes and goes, like hearts," becomes his "love-cars. Lights turned down" and " 'Love, O careless Love.' " Having begun with the season of year, a little over halfway through they narrow to her "Last night" and his "One dark night." Her poem climaxes "behind the house" with an armadillo holding its "tail down," a baby rabbit's "ignited eyes" and a *"piercing cry / and panic."* His ends "on top / of our back steps" with a skunk that "drops her ostrich tail" and leads its babies with "eyes' red fire" amidst "my ill-spirit sob."

The big difference comes in Lowell's explicit presence in his own poem; instead of making his skunk stand in for himself the way Bishop, absent from her poem in any explicit way, puts her own rage in the armadillo, Lowell sets the skunk against himself, even if only to imply that, colloquially speaking, he's more a skunk than the skunk. His *own* spirit sobs, the fragility is all Lowell's; whereas Bishop leaves the *"piercing cry"* to her well-plated animal, and enters the poem herself only if we *deduce* that it's she whom its cry pierces. She complains about people who launch fire balloons and make war and go mad, and about her friend Lowell, and only obliquely about that larger group that she belongs to of people who fall in and out of love. He, by contrast, pays homage to his friend Bishop by echoing her poem, and complains about himself overtly. She describes the fall of balloons, and vaguely implies that they bear some relation to the larger failures of us all. He, more bluntly, confesses his own fall ("my mind's not right"), romanticizing himself as some new avatar of Milton's Satan, whose words he repeats exactly: "myself am hell."

Thus that gap in Bishop's poem between the trivial damage that provokes her final plea and the intensity of the plea itself, the gap that makes the ending seem so oddly, perhaps awkwardly urgent, reappears in Lowell's poem with a striking difference, one that reveals much about both poems. For Lowell the skunk is ordinary. Rather than taking on his rage as the armadillo takes on Bishop's, it remains half-terrifyingly, half-reassuringly independent of him. He can't even scare it, which underlines its independence—and his own helpless weakness. For Lowell, the gap between cause and effect is all in himself, in his own inexplicable onset of insanity and his temptation to kill himself ("as if my hand were at its throat"). He desperately searches the world around him—Nautilus Island, the love-cars, the skunk—for some reassurance, some explanation for his loss of control, some way to fill in that gap. Bishop, then, puts the emotions in others, and to do that she must actively force them away, dissociate them, from herself. By contrast, Lowell, passively, finds the emotions *are* forced, dissociated, from he knows not where, but appallingly onto himself.

By taking onto himself or finding in himself what Bishop foists onto others, onto even such an innocent as the armadillo, Lowell exposes what Bishop disguises. In a sense, perhaps, it is easier for him—not to live through, but to acknowledge. He has Bishop to respond to, and he has before him the undisguisable fact of his mania, for which he was repeatedly hospitalized. Bishop's disguises are deft; a generation of readers saw her almost entirely as a poet of gentility. But once we lift that mask, she appears as a poet who studies the futility of disguise. Not even the armadillo's armor plates can protect it from its transparency as an embodiment of her rage; nor, presumably, would she want them to. Beauty, whether natural or from artifice, can disguise the traumas of place and mind, but not perfectly. The fire balloons rise in the sky, the landscape of Brazilian forest dazzles the explorers' eyes, but sooner or later the disasters show up: the explorers' stolen pleasures give birth to a new and dependent culture, the owls' shrieks draw our eyes to their burned nest, Lowell finds himself mad. No beauty can hide the inevitable. The most elaborately figured, most decorously deferred inevitable of "The Armadillo" is death: the near death of the baby rabbit and the armadillo; the death that fire bombs rained on Germany; the death of love ("that comes and goes"); the death—"splattered like an egg of fire"—of the owls' brood in their burned nest; the other death that the same egg-splattering figures, of the child Bishop will never have, and in particular never have—despite her occasional fantasy of it[27]—with Lowell. Bishop is hardly the first to find disguise a helpful way to face or not face the fear of death.

That same fear, and the mixed wish to face it and disguise it, she faces the most squarely in "First Death in Nova Scotia." "In the cold, cold parlor," begins "First Death in Nova Scotia," "my mother laid out Arthur / beneath the chromographs" of British royalty, which she itemizes one by one before adding that

> Below them on the table
> stood a stuffed loon
> shot and stuffed by Uncle
> Arthur, Arthur's father.

In this way, the poem opens with a child's little inventory, with an assortment of things Bishop might choose to develop. So far we have a coldness, and one rendered as rather oppressive and awesome by the slow, formal feeling that comes from repeating "cold" twice in succession, with the long *o* and liquid *l* sounds that take awhile to say, especially when doubled and made ponderous by repetition. And we have one particular character, Arthur, who in several ways seems to be the focus. She identifies her uncle by his relation to Arthur ("Arthur's father") rather than through his relation to her mother. Arthur, by contrast, she names directly, and in the first sentence, without explaining his relation to anyone else. She makes him the object of that sentence, and puts more emphasis on object than on subject, as the issue is what gets done to Arthur, not who does it. The three other characters, so far, appear incidentally: the mother to explain how Arthur got there, the first-person speaker to put some marker of explanation on the mother ("*my* mother"), and Uncle Arthur—marked like the mother by a first-person tag (to call him "Uncle" is to call him *my* uncle)—to explain how the loon got there. We also have the chromographs (early color photographs), respectfully detailed by naming each royal personage individually, though according to tacit assumptions of hierarchy: "Edward, Prince of Wales, / with Princess Alexandra, / and King George with Queen Mary." The child sees the royal women in secondary relation to the royal men. And we have the loon.

The remarkable thing about all this is that it gives us so much interesting material, but once she gets to the loon, it takes over. She makes us want to hear about the other, more dramatic things, the death of Arthur or the mother's role in presenting Arthur's death to the child. Next to such things, it is hard to think the loon matters. Still, the next stanza sticks tenaciously to that loon, but in an extra-ordinarily unextraordinary tone: "Since Uncle Arthur fired / a bullet into him, / he hadn't said a word." Those three lines are a triumph of quietness, astounding in what they show the first-person voice refusing to see, and at the same time immensely complicated, because to refuse to see something is, after a fashion, to see it. Else, why refuse? Indeed, why *would* he say a word? We easily believe he hasn't spoken, but it would never occur to us to say so—we take it so for granted. Her troubling to remark such a thing lets it slip out

that she doesn't understand it's not remarkable. She doesn't understand the most rudimentary circumstances of death.

So that even while the poem lingers irritatingly on that almost
irrelevant loon, its irritating irrelevance gives it, poignantly, a re-
cuperating relevance. It hangs before her like a slate onto which she
can safely project what really troubles her: the death of little Arthur.
At Arthur's death, or especially at his funeral—the time set aside
to take in his death—the loon suddenly magnetizes her, both because
it gives her something to think about that feels less painful than
thinking about Arthur, and because, indirectly, it lets her think about
Arthur nevertheless.

The connection is so strong and so strange and yet, like most
defenses, so natural, that I have heard many readers say they thought
for awhile that the Uncle fired his bullet into Arthur, and that's why
Arthur died. Syntactically, their misreading seems like one that Bishop
courts; the antecedent of "him" might as well be Arthur as the loon,
and only farther into the stanza do we get anything that unquestionably refers to the bird rather than the boy—unquestionably, but
not unambiguously:

> He kept his own counsel
> on his white, frozen lake,
> the marble-topped table.
> His breast was deep and white,
> cold and caressable;
> his eyes were red glass,
> much to be desired.

Surely Bishop knows we are more likely to think of Arthur keeping
his own counsel than of a stuffed loon's doing so. She uses her child's
perspective toyingly, shaping the poem from her adult perspective
to get both what the child knows it thinks about the loon and, through
the same words, what the child doesn't know it thinks about its little
cousin. By saying the excessively obvious, the little girl's perspective
conveys her naiveté. But it is a worried naiveté, for she would not
snag her attention on these things that adults assume unless she
suspected and resisted some pressure to assume them herself. It seems
as if, regarding the loon's death, the pressure never worried her
before. That lets her release onto the less threatening loon the new

pressure from what she feels asked to think about Arthur. Hence, gazing through the child's mind as well as at it, we see a discreet sophistication in the poet's overarching adult perspective, as if the adult were winking at us to confirm our shared but superior knowledge that these are strangely obvious things to say. The obvious truth about the dead loon, that never mattered to the child before, feels less obvious about Arthur. If we have even no more than a small doubt about the blurry referent, her mentioning the lake would seem to key it to the loon. But deftly, Bishop turns right from lake to table, much more the scene of boy than of bird, thus restoring, just barely, that remnant of doubt that most readers probably, by that point, find hard to take seriously but that many still find it hard to be rid of. Only when we reach the glass eyes does it become the loon for sure. Even then, though, the emotion she invests in the loon remains more convincingly her emotion for Arthur, now bewilderingly reft of its object and desperately redirected onto the loon. The loon doesn't seem to mind. It even attracts attention by its puzzling resemblance to the lost little boy, with its breast "deep and white, / cold and caressable," and its eyes "much to be desired." We know, as the little girl does not, the appeal of figuring out that puzzling loon, for we can see that she senses, without understanding, that if she can figure out the loon, then she can figure out Arthur.

The mother wants her to figure out Arthur, but not if figuring out Arthur will hurt, which of course it will. She lifts up the little girl, giving the first clear indication just how little she really is, and physically setting into conventional pattern the girl's not yet predictable reaction (and perhaps asserting control over her daughter's reaction as a way to claim control over her own). It seems she wants to explain, to assist her daughter's approach to the mystery of death, and yet that she fears explaining, because the explanation might hurt. So she compromises, interrupting the child's reverie to direct it, to socialize it into public ritual. For ritual can mediate mystery, whether we understand the mystery or not. " 'Come' said my mother, / 'Come and say good-bye / to your little cousin Arthur.' " The mother's words bring out her mix of impulses. On the one hand, she urges the girl closer to Arthur's corpse, the embodiment of evaded truth. On the other hand, her compromise, in effect, amounts to a lie. When she asks her daughter to address the corpse as if it could hear her, she urges her away from its truth even as, physically, she presses her closer to it. Sure enough, the boost from the mother does its work. It snaps the daughter away from her hypnotized blurring of Arthur and the loon:

> Arthur's coffin was
> a little frosted cake,
> and the red-eyed loon eyed it
> from his white, frozen lake.

When the child says that the loon eyes Arthur, she breaks the identification she had drifted into between bird and boy. Yet even that growth in knowledge Bishop brilliantly takes back by making her think that the dead loon eyes anything at all. Indeed, the girl announces her new knowledge in a way that defends against it by insisting—as children do—on some other feature of the old knowledge that it discredits. Thus even as she gives up projecting her cousin onto the loon, she still denies death, both her cousin's and the loon's. She assimilates her cousin's death into something reassuringly ordinary, into what she already associates with self-consciously ritualized social and family gatherings: "a little frosted cake."[28] The crisp rhyme of "cake" with "lake," all the crisper for being the first really strong rhyme in the poem and for coming at the stanza's end, stamps a finish on all these changes and defenses. It reinforces the newly won opposition between Arthur and the bird, the cake boy and the lake loon. And yet the pat comparison and sudden rhyme give off the sparks of a suspiciously large effort. They sound defensive: the candied metaphor sugarcoats Arthur's death, and the rhyme's abruptness suggests a trumped-up confidence. Both imply that she wants to stop right there, short of the doubt that intrigues but frightens her.

Through all this, the double reverberation of child's and adult's voices sorts out across the structural axis of any autobiographical act, that blend of participant's dissolving naiveté and rememberer's maturer knowledge that shapes narrative recollection from Augustine and Rousseau through *Great Expectations* and beyond. In this case, the child's immediate perplexity holds the foreground, while the adult poet's encompassing vision, though just as powerful, remains only implied. The sorting out of reminiscence and the staring at death especially recall Dickinson's manner in her poem 389:

There's been a Death, in the Opposite House,
As lately as Today —
I know it, by the numb look
Such Houses have — alway —

The Neighbors rustle in and out —
The Doctor — drives away —
A Window opens like a Pod —
Abrupt — mechanically —

Somebody flings a Mattress out —
The Children hurry by —
They wonder if it died — on that —
I used to — when a Boy —[29]

Unlike Bishop, Dickinson sees no corpse. She recognizes death by interpreting its signs ("It's easy as a Sign," she says later), by recognizing its displacement onto *things* and hushed reactions: a mattress, a rustling, a window opened mechanically, a frightened flinging away and hurrying by. All this identifies the subject less as death than as our response to it. We curl up under a shield of numbness, reifying whatever might otherwise prompt the pains and fears that death excites. Dickinson's speaker has no authentic access to what the children, whom "he" sees as hurrying by, might think. He simply decides (which is not to say he's wrong, or right) that the way they go by violates their ordinary pattern, and that the violation shows a fearful wondering, in an extraordinary series of phrases, "if it died — on that — / I used to — when a Boy —." The hardening into that pronoun *it* for a moment makes body and mattress indistinguishable, culminating the defensive reifying of the body. But mattresses do not die; *it* must refer to the body. Still, the body is not a corpse, not an it, until *after* dying. That is, *it* does not die; rather, *he* or *she* dies, someone "in the Opposite House" "In just a Country Town," and therefore someone nameable by automatic, unthinking reflex. That the corpse is not named, then, shows the speaker's intense thinking and worrying, right from the protectively casual, newsy opening line. Whoever it is, the speaker feels hurt that it is that particular person, and reifying her or him into "it" deflects a little of the pain.

The dashes redouble that evasion by the way they funnel attention in separate and competing directions. Were there no pause between "died" and "on that," the weight would fall on the children's wondering where the neighbor died—no great matter. But the dash makes us hesitate on "died," and then jump away as if from something hot, because the recognition of death hurts. We land at "on that," which, cut off by the dash from "died," works less to give the place of death than to replace the emphasis on death with an emphasis on "that," the mattress, set off by another dash. The dashes trip up the sentence on the suddenly tainted object's horrifying finality, as if the mattress stands in for the corpse that stands in for the person, frightfully objectifying the person's approaching fate by getting flung out. Flinging out the mattress frightens the speaker because it seems the neighbors would really like to fling out the corpse. And they do, though with the mediating, ritualized assistance of doctor, minister, milliner, and undertaker, who offend the speaker because they appropriate the neighbors' grief as if it were a reified thing indeed, the undertaker coming "to take the measure of the House" and the minister acting "As if . . . He owned all the Mourners—now."

Dickinson's speaker makes more explicit what Bishop's speaker feels but cannot understand. Both fear confronting the corpse's death, and focus on something material instead, the loon, or the mattress. Material things appeal because things cannot feel, and hence seem to promise some protection from the onrush of emotion, and from mutability itself, which death has so strongly placed before them. But the material things they turn to bear a connection to the dead people—the mattress by contiguity, the loon by analogy. That is why they turn to those particular things, but the same connections that attract them also send their attention looping right back to the death that threatened them in the first place. The speakers differ, though, in that Dickinson's is less naive. He satirizes the way other people around him publicly act out the nervous reifying that he turns to more privately. Bishop's little girl, by contrast, abides by what others think, allows herself to be told what to do and physically lifted into position to do it.

Still, Dickinson's narrator, despite his insight into others, understands his own defenses no better than Bishop's does. His defensive reifying troubles him enough to make him cough out those dashes, but, he insists, that's kids' stuff, and he's outgrown it: "The Children hurry by— / They wonder if it died—on that— / I used to—

when a Boy—." It is hard to come upon the word "Boy" without feeling startled. But again the dashes tell everything, and a comparison can help disclose the related worries of Bishop's less radical strategies.[30]

Given the pattern of defenses throughout Dickinson's poem, the conversion of emotions into objects, and the castigating satire of the townspeople who act out the same defenses (though, to be sure, more publicly and at a profit), the choice to speak in a male voice calls for more than ordinary scrutiny. It has no particular contextual motivation; nothing that the speaker says or does has to do with being male or female. And Dickinson hordes the fact of her speaker's gender for half the poem, setting us up so that we more or less innocently build expectations either of gender's irrelevance or of the speaker's femininity. It seems, then, either that she wants to criticize those expectations, or that she herself feels threatened by those expectations in herself. In other words, in some sense she decides to be male only after the poem gets going; changing to or adopting maleness eases some threat in the poem. Since gender doesn't otherwise play much of a role in this particular poem (though it does in many of her others), the threat seems not in her femininity but rather in her identification with the speaker. She changes gender, in other words, not so much to impersonate masculinity (as, say, in poem 986, "A narrow Fellow in the Grass," though other things come into play there as well), as to distance herself from the speaker. Something that "he" feels disturbs her.

It seems fitting, then, that "he" slips in a reference to his maleness immediately after identifying most closely with the feelings that Dickinson apparently finds offensive. The phrase "They wonder" puts the onus on others, on 'them.' But the speaker wonders too, and so gets caught up in a hesitating dash. Then she (as I'll call her for now, since that's my point) stumbles onto "on that," pausing for another dash that rests the objectifying weight on *that* and so lets out her own wonder, as she feels compelled to acknowledge—"I used to," stripped down now only to the defense of putting it in the past. But that gets too close to the hurtful truth, so she coughs up yet another dash, and then drops in a disclaimer—"when a Boy"— that rescues her from complicity by putting it all off on someone definitively not herself, someone male. Such distancing in the poet fits exactly the strategies that the poet gives her speaker. He feels hurt by the death of his neighbor, objectifies the pain, and projects his own objectifying onto the other townspeople. What he does to his grief, Dickinson does to some related grief of her own. She foists her defensive distancing onto him just as he foists his onto the neighbors, the children, and the officious functionaries.

The point is that both Dickinson and Bishop craft speakers mixed oddly of child's and adult's perspectives, and confront them with the death of someone who matters to them, which hurts and mystifies them so much that they displace their feelings onto objects and activities. Both seem uneasy with the social rituals designed to receive those displacements in a communally sanctioned forum. They work their griefs through privately, so far as the poems take us, even though they must do so against the background of other people's public accommodation. Dickinson, or her speaker, goes so far as to project her wish to treat emotions like things onto other people who, at least from her window's distance, look less sincere. She thus shifts to others, to a male speaker as well as to the townspeople, what she at least makes it seem are her own feelings. Given the two poems' many similarities of incident and tone, the greater extremes that Dickinson goes to can alert us to the possibility that Bishop confronts other people's responses more anxiously than we might notice.[31]

She can focus on the loon only for so long. When her mother lifts her up to talk to Arthur and hand him a lily, her attention is forced to settle on the corpse she fears. But even then, instead of acknowledging the trauma of Arthur's change or her pain at his inertness, she tames the corpse's threat by likening it to something she plays with every day, a doll. In some fashion, the adults have told her of death. She absorbs the word, presumably, but has more trouble absorbing what it means, its referent. The closest she gets is the touching unarbitrariness of the objects she fixes on to distract her from that corpse or to translate it to something more familiar: the loon, once alive and now dead; a doll, lifelike but never alive; or those chromographs of the royal family. Photographs seize the quick and make it still. They are icons of mortality, of what people once were and will never be again,[32] all the more so, perhaps, when they peer down in the sickly hue of chromographs. Thus at the poem's end, those chromographs that the girl had left behind in the first stanza suddenly have a lot to do with understanding Arthur's death:

> The gracious royal couples
> were warm in red and ermine;
> their feet were well wrapped up
> in the ladies' ermine trains.
> They invited Arthur to be
> the smallest page at court.
> But how could Arthur go,
> clutching his tiny lily,
> with his eyes shut up so tight
> and the roads deep in snow?

They are red and white and still, just like Arthur; but they are warm and he is ominously cold, cold, all through the poem. Then wouldn't he want to go join them? So she thinks, with childish logic, perhaps. But perhaps the childish logic is not hers. The notion of "the smallest page at court" sounds more like what a condescendingly gentle adult would tell a naive little child than like what this naive child would concoct by herself.[33] We are left to deduce that the gentle liar must be the mother, not only because she is the only candidate the poem actually refers to, but also because the poem has already shown the mother struggling, condescendingly and not altogether gracefully, to help her daughter adjust to Arthur's death.

The mother's role, thus described, gains yet more interest if we juxtapose "First Death in Nova Scotia" with "Filling Station," its facing poem in *Questions of Travel* and both editions of collected poems, and with "In the Village," which Bishop gave special emphasis by making it the only prose in *Questions of Travel*. In chapter one, we have already discussed the curious pride and uneasiness about the invisible but still interpretable mother in "Filling Station," and "In the Village" describes how slightly Bishop knew her mother and how traumatically she lost her. To the extent that we take "First Death in Nova Scotia," then, as the autobiography it wears the guise of, we are left to guess that Bishop has displaced her grandmother with a fictional poetic mother.[34] In the various prose stories ("Gwendolyn," "In the Village," "Memories of Uncle Neddy," "Primer Class"[35]) her grandmother figures about like the mother in "First Death," but her mother is gone in every story except "In the Village," where she comes and seems distressingly unfamiliar and then quickly and memorably goes "forever," in the word—perhaps not coincidentally—that Bishop applies twice, and both times with emphasis, to Arthur. Bishop feels some need to place her more or less fictionalized past in terms of the mother she was denied. Yet when she resuscitates her mother in "First Death," she brings her back only to reject her, for the poem ends as the little girl starts to realize that what her mother, or at least the adult world her mother partly represents, has told her about death has somehow implausibly sweetened the story.

Inclined, at first, to trust what the big people have told her, she finds it hard to doubt that Arthur really will go "to be / the smallest page at court," but she cannot help doubting anyway, because it seems so unlikely (in the apt word of "In the Waiting Room") that he can get there. Bishop brings out the pathos of childhood bewilderment by ending not with the implausibility of Arthur's dead body doing anything, not, that is, with what would make his journey unlikely to adults, but instead with the more ordinary impediments of closed eyes and winter snow. As in so many of her poems, a suddenly strong rhyme in the last syllable gives an odd emphasis and finality to that last, cold, cold word, "snow." With cool silence, the adult perspective gives way entirely, at the end, to the child's thoughts to itself, no longer softened by recollected description, and thus leaving all alone the irony of childish credibility, as the child resists the tug of mortality that it nevertheless feels.

That lonely childish perplexity recalls the ending of a story in many ways very similar, Hemingway's "Indian Camp." With intensely compressed and suggestive prose, "Indian Camp" recounts a small child's abrupt encounter with death. Hemingway's style could well have influenced Bishop's tendency to suggestive understatement; it at least helped create an audience ready to read Bishop. In the last paragraph and sentence of Hemingway's story, young Nick Adams, apparently a few years older than Bishop's very young child, reaches for a final thought about his sudden immersion in final things: "In the early morning on the lake sitting in the stern of the boat with his father rowing, he felt quite sure that he would never die."[36] And there the story ends. We might conclude from such an ending that both Nick and the young girl in Bishop's poem refuse to let death diminish their confidence in immortality; readers sometimes think that Nick's final thought shows he has learned nothing from his introduction to death. But Nick's optimism exposes its own fragility. He would not trouble to think that he will never die unless some part of him felt very powerfully that he will die for sure. Where a traditional story concludes with a change or with new knowledge in the major character, Hemingway varies that principle just enough to hold onto it in subtler fashion. Instead of giving us the change, he gives the grounds for change, and then suddenly stops with the poor character's wounded resentment of the change about to come. The change itself he leaves out; to the war-weary, post-*bildungs-roman* world of 1925 it would seem only some lusterless cliché of newly won maturity. The real drama lies in the circumstances of change and in Nick's sense of being so stymied by those circumstances that, to resist his dawning sense of futility, he grasps after a dream of constancy and immunity.

Just as Nick clutches after a new fantasy, the young child of "First Death in Nova Scotia" clings to an old one. Either way, the effect is about the same: the sudden ending in implausible confidence dramatizes that the children no longer believe their own self-deceptions. Nor can they continue to believe in their parents' power to temper their fears. Hemingway's little boy and Bishop's little girl have begun to sense that his father's boasting and her mother's reassurance are both bluffs. The adults do not really believe in their own professions of complacency, and their children are becoming like them, are changing or about to change into unbelievers.

But why does Bishop insist, in her title, on Nova Scotia? What has that to do with the child's change? Nova Scotia is the last scene of her innocence. She latches on to something especially Nova Scotian, "the roads deep in snow," as a less threatening explanation for Arthur's stillness. He holds still because the snow will not let him go. It makes a feeble explanation, as feeble as Nick's confidence in his immortality, but that is Bishop's point. Nova Scotia, as the stories she sets there make especially clear, is the land of the childhood she lost and will never recover, and this poem records her discovery of that childhood's mortality. The little girl fixes on the geographical obstacles that make the adults' story about Arthur hard to believe. Regardless of where Arthur actually goes, though, she can see she is not ready to follow. But she cannot stay in her own place either; Arthur's death has changed it forever, made it, in effect, another place. When Bishop leaves Nova Scotia, then, she leaves not only the literal place but, already this early, she begins to leave the innocence that Nova Scotia metaphorizes. Place can never again give her refuge from unbelief; not even Nova Scotia can save her innocence. For this is, after all, only her first death in Nova Scotia. There will be many more. But even now that Nova Scotia has changed, it will always represent for her the place where for a while she did not know death. She can never return to it—she must move on, she must travel. Even before she leaves the physical place, she has left forever the metaphorical place, because she can no longer believe in it. Instead of believing in one place, she will pass the remainder of her life traveling restlessly from one place to another, at home in the *idea* of place but not in any particular place so much as in a feeling of unbelief and disillusion.

No one, perhaps, could make a better figure of disillusion for an American poet in the 1950s than Ezra Pound, who sought to save the world and—in lieu of standing trial and risking execution for treason—ended up in the radically circumscribed world of St. Elizabeths hospital for the insane. "Visits to St. Elizabeths," one of Bishop's best poems, seems missing from discussions of her poetry almost the way the "The Pied Piper of Hamelin" usually escapes criticism of Robert Browning. Everybody likes it, but it seems so quirkily frolicsome and even juvenile that hardly anyone says anything about it. One suspects a difficulty in taking the poem seriously. Perhaps it gets mentioned so rarely because it seems to have little in common with her other poems. Or, more narrowly, because it has little in common with what people have written about the others; that is, it has none of the other poems' startling reticence and compression, and less of their lingering in precise description. But if there is more than that in Bishop's other poems, as I have been claiming, then perhaps there is more also in "Visits to St. Elizabeths." Indeed, like Browning's "Pied Piper," written for children, and like so many classic children's tales, Bishop's poem, based on the nursery rhyme "This is the house that Jack built," is full of fright and melancholy.

Somehow she aims all the poem's swirl of alarm and sadness at Pound. To comment on Pound in the late forties and the fifties became a national ritual of political passion and—or often *or*— aesthetic principle. The political judgments (by all but the occasional fanatic) were radically dismissive at their gentlest. Newspapers wrote openly that Pound should be shot. Many writers felt that Pound, as a great writer, deserved lenience; writers organized Pound's defense and got him declared unfit to stand trial and committed to the lunatic asylum. There he eventually was visited by a mixed stream of the cultural elite and the racist riffraff—sometimes as many as fifteen people at once would wait to see him.[37] To judge Pound was to judge not only one poet but also the relation between poetry and the culture at large. If Pound did or did not deserve special treatment on account of his poetry, or on account of his service to other writers (possibly greater than any other single person's in this century), then that said something larger about the nature of justice or the cultural role of art. So whatever Bishop says about Pound has to do with much more than just the strange doyen of one hospital for the insane.

Indeed, she does not begin with Pound at all. "This is the house of Bedlam," she begins, strikingly less personal than "This is the house that Jack built," though the nursery rhyme's echo hints that some Jack, some single person, might bear responsibility for the madness. But she never mentions Pound by name. Instead, the next line and stanza introduce him—to those who happen to recognize the title's reference to Pound's hospital—as "the man":

> This is the man
> that lies in the house of Bedlam.
>
> This is the time
> of the tragic man
> that lies in the house of Bedlam.

Here Bishop starts to suggest an attitude to her unnamed iconoclast. He is "the man / that lies." Anyone who recognizes St. Elizabeths as a hospital is likely to imagine Pound, as patient, woefully confined and recumbent, which wins our sympathy. His visitors, though, saw that before long he led a lively, industrious, and even crowded life in the hospital, indulged by the staff and, after the first year, finding himself in a relatively decent room, free of financial worry for the first time in his life. Such details ask us to let the other meaning of "lies" rise more and more prominently, especially as the poem's form makes Bishop repeat the word eleven times in twelve stanzas. Sad case though he was, Pound could not be trusted. She could have said "the man / *who* lies," but she distances him by an impersonal pronoun. Not till the third stanza does she get more specific, giving

him an adjective, "tragic," the first in a series that points each
following stanza to judgment: "tragic," "talkative," "honored," "old,
brave," "cranky," "cruel," "busy," "tedious," "the poet, the man,"
and "wretched."[38] Such descriptions make a complicated commentary, at once—or perhaps in alternation—admiring and critical,
pitying and neutrally descriptive. Amidst the praise, though, the
criticism rings soberly: cranky, cruel, tedious, and wretched. No one
except a few neo-Nazis could visit Pound and hear his obstinate,
hateful diatribes on politics and economics, race and religion without
recognizing that, regardless of how the courts might rule, he was in
some sense both crazy and guilty. And Bishop finds nothing ro-
mantically poetic in insanity.[39]

Bishop's disgust with Pound shows more clearly when we realize
that the nursery rhyme would not have been her only source. Coleridge, in the *Biographia Literaria*, a book Bishop much admired,
had already done another version of "This is the house that Jack
built," which Bishop would surely have known. Coleridge calls his
sonnet a self-parody ("And this reft house is that, the which he built,
/ Lamented Jack!"), mocking his own "indiscriminate use of elaborate and swelling language and imagery."[40] A similar mockery carries
over to Bishop's treatment of Pound, even when we do not know
the minor Coleridge piece, as she reduces the emperor of the erudite
to a nursery rhyme, and suggests that the house of his decay, his
descent to St. Elizabeths, is of his own building. His pretensions to
be grander than anyone else and grander in some special, more than
poetic way mark him as just another of the very people he would
most claim superiority to:

> a boy that pats the floor
> to see if the world is there, is flat,
> for the widowed Jew in the newspaper hat
> that dances weeping down the ward
> waltzing the length of a weaving board.

The form's repetition enables Bishop, uncoincidentally, to mention
a Jewish patient, and refer to him as a Jew, five times. Given Pound's
anti-Semitism and its relation to his troubles, that underscores the
irony of his common fate with his present companions.

Her form also calls for each stanza to begin differently, but Bishop
opens two stanzas by saying "These are the years." Pound, in other

he is stuck for a long stay. "These are the years" and "This is the time." His incarceration starts tragically to represent what Bishop elsewhere called "our worst century so far."[41] It is our time, not just his—the Pound Era, as Hugh Kenner later dubbed it, where the world still sputters in the shadow of Pound's once-triumphant literary Modernism and the cataclysm it got swept up in, sweeping Pound along with it. By 1950, Pound has become identified with that cataclysm's aftermath. This is, then, a postwar poem, intent on the war's human refuse: sailor, soldier, traitor.

Yet in an odd way it remains a personal as well as a public poem. Bishop could have titled it any number of things without suggesting a connection to her own name. Somehow these are visits to herself or to some idealized (sainted) version of herself; and somehow she encompasses Pound, becomes the place or the sphere in which he lies condemned. Pound seemed to many people the priest of language—especially poetic language—at its most pristine; and though he himself saw poetry as worldly and political, his advocates after the war were reduced to dismissing his political significance so that they could defend him on the grounds of a poet's exalted privilege. In that sense Pound represents an idealized form of the poet Bishop aspires to be herself. But of course it cannot be so simple; his very place in the hospital testifies to the lie in his alleged purity and independence, so that he degrades the very exaltation of poetry that he also represents. Bishop, meanwhile, plays the saintly, condescending role of generous but pitying visitor. And as she visits Pound, she visits also a potential for aesthetic self-exaltation that, unlike Pound, she declines. In her generosity, then, she becomes larger than even the great Pound, diminished as he is by petty hates and partialities. She encompasses him in her poem, and in doing so she confines him, she defeats him by mastering and enclosing him. It is like her anguished taunt to Lowell in "The Armadillo," the next poem she published, where she fears some treacherous connection between his kind of art and his madness, and indicates that the art, much as she admires it, comes out tainted. Pound's art does the same; and it was Lowell, perhaps in more ways than one, who first took her to visit Pound at St. Elizabeths.[42]

From Pound's tainted art Bishop keeps a certain distance, even as she acknowledges her admiration for it. Her bouncy, nursery-rhyme dactyls mixed with occasional anapests make a jaunty rhythm

that keeps her from identifying with Pound, even under circumstances that might seem to call for it. The oddness of the rhythm
for such a subject shows the more by contrast with poems from
Lowell's *Life Studies* on similar subjects: the still, ironically quiet
rhythm in "Skunk Hour" as Lowell feels himself going mad, the
self-romanticizing wit in "Memories of West Street and Lepke" as
he measures his middle age against his youthful idealism and the
jail it led him to, and his actual confinement—almost like Pound's—
in a madhouse in "Waking in the Blue." Not surprisingly, "Waking
in the Blue" actually echoes "Visits to St. Elizabeths," but because
Lowell speaks in his own voice and about himself, the similar words
work a different effect. When he opens by describing his surroundings
and mentioning "The night attendant, a B.U. sophomore," and then
concludes the first stanza with the parenthetical explanation, prac-
tically a quotation of Bishop "(This is the house for the 'mentally
ill')," the joke collapses on him, self-exposed as the Harvard professor
reduced to being guarded by that B.U. sophomore with his head
drowsily "propped on *The Meaning of Meaning*."

Like Lowell, Anne Sexton also echoes "Visits to St. Elizabeths."
In "Ringing in the Bells," written about the same time as "Waking
in the Blue," she too uses Bishop's words to describe her own time
in the asylum. "And this is the way they ring / the bells in Bedlam,"
Sexton begins. For both Sexton and Lowell, the repetition of Bishop
turns around ironically to take us closer to the voices of Bedlam,
which now speak for themselves and seem so interior after the
impersonal, visitor's voice of Bishop's poem. Sexton repeats the words
from Bishop's more formal opening line, but uses them to set up a
shock when her next lines turn casually to the first person and
colloquial: "and this is the bell-lady / who comes each Tuesday
morning / to give us a music lesson." Similarly, Lowell adds a gritty
particularity when, a little later in the poem, he once more echoes
the loftier sound of Bishop's opening line, "This is the way day
breaks in Bowditch Hall at McLean's." Even the name of his insti-
tution, "ditch" and all, has a grimy immediacy to it, whereas Bishop's
"St. Elizabeths" carries a romantic and mythic sound, not at all
fitting its function.[43]

Bishop has a motive for visiting Pound and yet keeping her distance
from him, a motive beyond anything that has to do merely with
Pound. Her visits to Pound cannot help calling to mind her mother's

commitment to a "house for the 'mentally ill,' " beginning with the crack-up so memorably recounted in "In the Village"—after which Bishop never saw her mother again, never visited her—and continuing until her death in 1934. Pound's reminder of her mother intensifies Bishop's distanced and defended-against identification with him. His fate matters especially to her because, as a poet, he represents a potential in herself, but also because he represents more that lies potential in herself than poetry alone. All of which redoubles the way Bishop's poem about Pound is partly and surreptitiously also a poem about herself, about her visits to St. *Elizabeths.*

Fittingly, then, she shows pride, as well as resentment, at what Pound represents. Many others would succumb to an easy dismissal or a contrivedly apolitical apology, but the comments in Bishop's last stanzas conclude much more maturely than that. In the third stanza from the end, she calls Pound "the tedious man." She rebukes him, but not with the usual kind of criticism that grants much significance to the foolishness it blames him for. And she recognizes also that Pound's achievement, however tainted, survives; he is, in the next to last stanza, "the poet, the man." Apologists might have stopped there, but in the last stanza Bishop adds one more adjective, a complicated one: "the wretched man." "Wretched" adds no more epithets to Pound's earlier triumphs or his remnant of dignity, to the career of "the poet, the man." Instead it describes the general state he has sunk to in 1950, despicable and yet, partly because so despicable, pitiable as well.

She describes Pound by the pathos of where she finds him, a sorry place, but in some ways a good place for a person who needs it. Place becomes her medium in "Visits to St. Elizabeths" as in the other most memorable poems of Bishop's middle career. She turns to place as her route to the self, a circuitous route compared to the more forthright paths of a Lowell or a Sexton, and a route that might seem to lead protectively away from the self, to leave the self, with its idiosyncrasies, less exposed and less at risk than the poems of *North & South.* At the same time, that she reaches the self by a long route should not lead us to think, as some readers have, that she never gets there at all. The title of "Visits to St. Elizabeths," with its mockery of her own "saintly" proprieties of persona, reminds us of the intensity in her indirect, reflected gaze at herself through the wretched image of Pound.

Lowell said that he worked out the informal, prosaic rhythms of *Life Studies* from reading Bishop.[44] And yet, prosaic though her verse usually seems, Bishop's circling path to the self gives her poems a formal feeling that, beginning with *Life Studies*, Lowell leaves behind. Her more traditional forms help keep her away from the flamboyant egotism that "The Armadillo" shows she feared in Lowell even before *Life Studies*. Even so, her later poems change, as if the intense personalism in the new poems of Lowell and others released her to explore private things more frankly. In the best of her later poems she turns less to examining the self through its surroundings. Still, she gets hardly more direct; she stays far from the confessional manner of Lowell, Berryman, or Sexton. "You just wish they'd keep some of these things to themselves," she said of Lowell's confessional imitators not long after she finished *Questions of Travel*.[45] Instead of turning to confessional directness, she confronts her present as indirectly as ever by looking back at her past almost the way she implicitly looks back at Pound's, but without the protective distance she keeps from him. Having written poems out of her own immediate wish, and then out of the places around her, late in life she turns back in retrospect to the wishes and places of her past.

CHAPTER FOUR

Retrospect: *Geography III*

Repeat, repeat, repeat; revise, revise, revise.
—"North Haven"

In "The Moose," Bishop begins on the axis of *place*, but settles in to prepare to leave, rather than to stay. She writes, in effect, an elegy for place, crossing from an axis of place to an axis of memory. That is, she crosses from the preoccupation of her middle career, at the beginning of which she saw the moose on a 1946 trip back from Nova Scotia,[1] to the preoccupation of her last collection, *Geography III* (1976), for which she finished "The Moose" twenty-six years later.

She begins in the exterior, describing the Nova Scotian and then the New Brunswick landscape in terms that recall "Cape Breton" (1949) of *A Cold Spring*, where she had written in oracular, pregnant intonations that "Whatever the landscape had of meaning appears to have been abandoned, / unless the road is holding it back, in the interior." Of course, she purports to mean the geographical interior, but "Cape Breton" so carefully confines itself to the landscape alone that, especially in light of "The Moose," the word "interior," as a sign of what the poem refrains from, starts to gather extra resonance and suggest a holding back from the bodily and emotional interior that erupted in "The Weed." Nevertheless, in 1949 she implies that, however barren the landscape appears, it is where we should search for meaning.

That changes twenty-three years later, in "The Moose," where, though Bishop lingers in landscape for fourteen stanzas, hovering for a last look at what she bids farewell, she also lets us know right away that she is leaving it. The meaning she seeks now lies elsewhere. "*From* narrow provinces," she begins (italics added), not in them. The landscape rests in stillness, with only a leisurely movement of water and sun—until her description reaches the bus that slices through the peaceful and perhaps even "femininely" pink repose, deflecting it with the harsh, bruised blue of metal and machine:

> the windshield flashing pink,
> pink glancing off of metal,
> brushing the dented flank
> of blue, beat-up enamel.

This bus takes people away from their homes. At one stop, Bishop renders their thoughts: "Goodbye to the elms, / to the farm, to the dog. / The bus starts." It takes them from the exterior of landscape and busyness to, as the evening meanders on, something interior:

> The passengers lie back.
> Snores. Some long sighs.
> A dreamy divagation
> begins in the night,
> a gentle, auditory,
> slow hallucination. . . .
>
> In the creakings and noises,
> an old conversation
> —not concerning us,
> but recognizable, somewhere,
> back in the bus.
>
>   ·   ·   ·   ·
>
> Now, it's all right now
> even to fall asleep
> just as on all those nights.

The interior world into which Bishop relaxes here is a world of permissions: it's all right now. Instead of leaving, now she can settle in, but this time into something other than place, other than land-scape—into some condition of memory and mind.

She leaves her readers to determine what condition, to ask "just as on" *what* nights. Without ever directly saying, she implies that she means the nights when, as a child, she fell asleep to the comforting rumblings of her grandparents' talk:

> back in the bus:
> Grandparents' voices
>
> uninterruptedly
> talking, in Eternity.

The place has changed. She lies no longer in her childhood's little village in Nova Scotia. But from a different place and a later time she turns back in retrospect to a past that the intervening years, and perhaps the nostalgia born of disappointment, make somehow special. In her imagination, place now yields to time, especially to memory. She concentrates less on what shows immediately around her, and more on what she can see in retrospect, what she can see—as if for the first time—perhaps because it's gone. The past is thus no longer passed; it transforms to the Eternal, with a capital *E*. Similarly, grandparents become Grandparents, not hers alone, but the idea of grandparents in general: those who, mythologized through memory, have diffused into the Eternal. Their voices drift from "somewhere / back in the bus" as from the irrecoverable recesses of recollection, from somewhere, then, back in the self.

It is not easy to hear things from somewhere, back in the self. But as Bishop rides on the bus, something special cracks the carapace between our origins and our selves. It comes partly from her return to the scene of her earliest associations; still, place in itself would not set off such feelings, or she would probably have felt them before in *A Cold Spring* and *Questions of Travel*. Her unaccustomed re-version to childhood mystery, now softened by the safety of adult distance, wells up not merely from place but also from the way that returning to—and then leaving again—the place of her past and her early childhood stirs up a crowd of associations that might never have slipped loose if she stayed either in Nova Scotia or away from it. The sleepy rhythm of the road and the bus helps release what she held within, just as it releases dream. For the memory she has buried inside is itself connected to falling asleep and probably to the dreamy release of feelings and thoughts that she and her talking grandparents would bury at any other time of day.

All this suggests something more largely primal than the merely personal run of her own earliest memories, though exactly what, it would be difficult and perhaps reductive to say. In this sleepy dream-time of associations let loose, things gain a peaceful finality that eludes us in the workaday world of wakefulness:

> things cleared up finally;
> what he said, what she said,
> who got pensioned;
>
> deaths, deaths and sicknesses;
> the year he remarried;
> the year (something) happened.
> She died in childbirth.
> That was the son lost
> when the schooner foundered.
>
> He took to drink. Yes.
> She went to the bad.
> When Amos began to pray
> even in the store and
> finally the family had
> to put him away.
>
> "Yes . . ." that peculiar
> affirmative. "Yes . . ."
>
> .   .   .   .
>
> that means "Life's like that.
> We know *it* (also death)."

In the way that sleep and memory can blot out or repress the conflicts in the same feelings they otherwise release from repression, this acquiescence to Eternity takes every unresolved thing and sifts it gently to conclusion. Bishop hangs with wonder over the finishing-off sound of "Yes." She says "finally," twice, and compresses her emotions into conclusively short sentences and phrases that lead each memory to its inexorable fate, and no further.

So that when "—Suddenly the bus driver / stops with a jolt" before the moose, the change and the beast that prompts it seem not altogether sudden. Rather, they pop up as if summoned by the hallucinated mix of final thoughts with first thoughts: grandparents evoke our beginnings, yet also, especially to a small child, they suggest a proximity to ends. In their sentimental nostalgia, then, these recollections hint at childhood's lively promise, but their urgency lies elsewhere. For one by one all these sentences walk the inescapable plank: "deaths, deaths and sicknesses," "she died in childbirth," "We know *it* (also death)." Thus the moose somehow embodies the obscure, elemental thoughts that the bus ride and its sleepy *longeurs* bring oddly together, including even death.

As the old people on the bus become her grandparents, she becomes both the small child in Nova Scotia and the adult in her sixties (whose companion of seventeen years has recently killed herself) who turns now to face her own death. The passage through geography merges with her passage through memory to whisper also of her passage through life to death, making a kind of before-the-fact elegy for herself. Indeed, her passage in the bus echoes Whitman's elegiac litany for Lincoln's passing to the "drooping star in the west" in "When Lilacs Last in the Dooryard Bloom'd," especially the famous section 5 with its long-delayed predicate:

Over the breast of the spring, the land, amid cities,
Amid lanes and through old woods, where lately the violets peep'd
  from the ground, spotting the gray debris,
Amid the grass in the fields each side of the lanes, passing the endless
  grass,
Passing the yellow-spear'd wheat, every grain from its shroud in the
  dark-brown fields uprisen,
Passing the apple-tree blows of white and pink in the orchards,
Carrying a corpse to where it shall rest in the grave,
Night and day journeys a coffin.[2]

Whitman's lines prepare us to hear the same sad note in Bishop's opening stanzas: "From narrow provinces / . . . where . . . / where . . / where . . . ; / on red, gravelly roads, / down rows of sugar maples, / past clapboard farmhouses / . . . past twin silver birches, / through late afternoon / a bus journeys west."

When the moose comes, then, it evokes the same elemental and natural world that death returns us to, but which, while still alive, we feel separate from. In that way, Bishop feels close to but separate from the moose. She peers at it interestedly, and yet still through the bus window's barrier, much as Frost's young couple in "Two Look at Two" look at their doe and buck across a barbed-wire fence that mocks their romantic assurance of oneness with Nature (and, more ominously, with each other). The moose's world is another, an "otherworldly" world, much more mysterious than Marianne Moore's " 'One looked at us / with its firm face part brown, part white—a queen / of alpine flowers. Santa Claus' reindeer, seen / at last.' " Unlike Moore, who transmits her report from a U.S. Education Bureau document and a "friend who'd been in Lapland,"[3] Bishop actually enters the moose's world, if a vision through the bus window counts. At least she fancies some special contact with it, but soon, in the last word of the poem, she returns to the mechanical, synthetic world of "gasoline."

In the meantime, though, the sudden "jolt" that interrupts Bishop's interior peace also exposes a hidden and complementary peace in the exterior world, outside the self and outside the bus. Bishop's tone and quiet drama plead strangely for profundity, a profundity that— as readers of Frost, especially poems like "Two Look at Two" and "The Most of It"—she, and her readers, must feel tempted to see skeptically. She refrains, however, from anthropomorphizing the moose, as Frost's young couple anthropomorphize the doe and buck. Bishop the unbeliever felt as wary of such sentimentalizing as Frost did. Not long after her bus trip, she praised Moore for seeing animals as themselves and not as people: "There are morals aplenty in animal life, but they have to be studied out by devotedly and minutely observing the animal, not by regarding the deer as a man imprisoned in a 'leathern coat.' "[4] And years later, not long before completing "The Moose," she translated Vinícius de Moraes's "Sonnet of Intimacy," which concludes by taking pleasure in animal company, but an amusing pleasure that he tries not to sentimentalize:

> The cattle look at me unenviously
> And when there comes a sudden stream and hiss
>
> Accompanied by a look not unmalicious,
> All of us, animals, unemotionally
> Partake together of a pleasant piss.

Still, if it were unemotional, he would not conclude a poem with it. Even Frost keeps returning to the natural world that he mocks our fascination with. At least Bishop's romanticism, like Frost's, recognizes the risk of sentimentalizing. She seems to sense that her romanticism has its origins in herself rather than in some inherent spirit of the natural world. Her encounter with the primeval in Nature links to and seems to grow from her encounter with the primeval in herself, so that the words she thinks to herself, immediately before the jolt of the moose, take on by the end a new force: "Now, it's all right now / even to fall asleep / just as on all those nights." Now, toward the end of her life, twenty-six years after she started to think about this poem, it's all right to abdicate wish, all right to leave place, all right, now, even to die.

The late poems of Bishop's career look back over her earlier life to see her present life afresh. As, early in her career, she wished for what she did not have, and then, more modestly expecting less, resigned herself to what lay immediately around her, so now, in the major poems from the end of her career she looks to see how where she has been and what she has wished for can help her discover at last what she is and, sometimes, has been all along. They are poems for the end of life, like the aptly titled "The End of March," or like "One Art" with its inventory of the many years' losses, and its dogged half-pretense that we grow accustomed to the pain.

"One Art" sarcastically meanders along through retrospect until it reaches the present in the last stanza, and then suddenly, in the last line, it breaks into wish.

> —Even losing you (the joking voice, a gesture
> I love) I shan't have lied. It's evident
> the art of losing's not too hard to master
> though it may look like (*Write* it!) like disaster.

The final line sputters through four anguished qualifications— "though," "may," "like," and then "like" again[5] and an almost involuntary spasm when for a moment her strained calm gives way to an interrupting and exclamatory imperative. Yet against all the imperative's energy, she cushions it carefully in parentheses and tucks it away in the line's middle. The intense knotting of emotion suggests that Bishop's vantage of retrospect no longer lets her believe in her wish. She wishes passionately, but after so many losses she hardly expects anything will come from it. Yet she must expect something, or she wouldn't write the last stanza, let alone insist on writing it. At the last, then, she grasps after the small hope that she can at least stretch out one last fuller hope by anticipating its collapse.

She gives up on the geography that anchored so many of her poems over the last twenty-five years, for she counts "place" and "where" among her losses: "places, and names, and where it was you meant / to travel," "two cities . . . , / some realms I owned, two rivers, a continent." Late in life her effort to recover wish sounds all the more poignant because at last she acknowledges her wish frankly, and acknowledges also her painfully accumulated confidence that it cannot work. "One Art" is a villanelle, and the repetitions of villanelle form intensify her sarcasm as she pretends that she can lightly toss off the pains from one disaster after another. With each repetition, a gradually confining inevitability closes in. Every "master" leads to "disaster," until we expect nothing else. Even her list of little losses sets up an ironic suspense as it makes us wait for larger ones to fulfill the sarcasm of "art" and "isn't hard to master." It is all too easy to "master" the "art" of losing, if to master it means to lose again and again, and all too difficult if to master it means to live through it artfully. In the meantime, though, the small losses gradually build up their own metaphorical resonance. From the ordinary bric-a-brac of daily disappearance she chooses "lost door keys," in themselves a metaphor of significance, of what is "key," and then she adds that she has lost her mother's watch. Indeed she has, living all her life away from her mother's eye, and showing the pain of that loss in poem after poem.

When in the last stanza she finally reaches the largest loss, or at least the imminent one that feels largest right then, she finds it hard to speak out. For it is no object or place, but instead a personality and a love, things that feel much harder to describe without some wrenching sense of distortion. Thus she gets most reticent at the same moment she also gets most explicit, caught up in the paradox of emotions deeply cherished and deeply feared. She parenthesizes personality, the "you" she loves, and parenthesizes also her desperate wish to *write* what she feels. Still, in the midst of all her unbeliever's frightened qualifications, she *does* write it, by writing this poem, the one art that gives her a hedge against loss. It cannot stop loss, but it can add something that helps make up for the losses that it records, anticipates, and pleads for one last respite from.

In "One Art," Bishop looks back from the evening of her life much as Crusoe looks back in another of her late poems, "Crusoe in England." As Crusoe feels mystified by the discovery that his life has disappointed him, so in "One Art" Bishop feels a corresponding pain but—writing a few years later—views it more wisely. She sees the pattern that bewilders him, the inexorable turn of every hope to despair, and yet she manages to hope—however slightly—that by recognizing the pattern she can forestall its next collapse upon her. "One Art" looks with fright from the past to the future, but "Crusoe in England" looks back only at the past. As Crusoe reviews his life, Bishop takes one of her rare steps into a voice clearly not her own; but unlike, say, Browning in his dramatic monologues— the first major poems of that tradition—she plainly adapts Crusoe's voice to her private preoccupations, though she still does so without compromising his independent (albeit fictional) authenticity.

Wondering what to make of his life and his past, Bishop's Crusoe (who hasn't much in common with Defoe's, outside of external circumstances) recalls how, even many years ago, back on his island, when he looked at the "miserable, small volcanoes,"

> I'd think that if they were the size
> I thought volcanoes should be, then I had
> become a giant;
> and if I had become a giant,
> I couldn't bear to think what size
> the goats and turtles were,
> or the gulls, or the overlapping rollers.

He has only his own world to judge by, but his world seems as if it might have changed as precipitously as Gulliver's changes from London to Lilliput. Not that he believes it did; he simply realizes that he can't tell whether it did or didn't. He is an unbeliever. Bishop draws again on her fascination with dizzying shifts of scale, with the vertigo we get from questioning our judgment, as in earlier poems like "The Man-Moth" and "Brazil, January 1, 1502," or in "12 O'Clock News" from *Geography III*.[6] One volcano, says Crusoe, "I'd christened *Mont d'Espoir* [Mount of Hope] or *Mount Despair* / (I'd time enough to play with names)." The two names are opposites, but for his purposes one name will do as well as the other; his isolation transforms meaning to an infinitely variable product of time rather than a constant. Instead of discovering meaning as authority, he produces it as play.

But he still looks at his production satirically, through a nostalgic yearning for the absolutes he once assumed. He cannot fully desert them until, after seeing the face of relativism, he returns to England's web of absolutes and finds that they no longer fit his retrospective fantasy of an easy and unthreatened confidence. It sounds like what might happen to a castaway in the seventeenth century, or simply like what might happen from growing up in the twentieth century. It sounds, in other words, like Crusoe—and like Bishop returning to North America after so many years in Brazil. So that when, back in England, he hears that a new volcano has erupted to make a newborn island, he thinks: "They named it. But my poor island's still / un-rediscovered, un-renamable. / None of the books has ever got it right." He announces their act of naming in a little pat sentence that suggests some mix of resignation to the finality "they" dictate and skepticism at their presumption, at the idea that anyone can author the finality that names supposedly hold.

Earlier, when he still believed in the authority his isolation starts to undermine, he lamented his loss of books, so "One of the first things that I did / when I got back was look" up something from a book. But England, it turns out, is equally an island. England's books bear no universal truth. The very word he looks up, "solitude" from Wordsworth's "bliss of solitude" (in "I Wandered Lonely as a Cloud"), comically fails, in Wordsworth's context, to fit Crusoe's own more troublesome solitude, or even, historically, to exist at all, since Wordsworth didn't write it for another hundred years. Thus the emotional and chronological inaptness of the word he focuses on redoubles his dizzying sense that he has lost a standard to judge by. He has only his unbeliever's lonely and bewildering sensations. His lost island is all too terribly his own, the unshareable, unreproducible product of—paradoxically—the perspective it gave him.[7]

Once an isolatoe, he is lonely forever, even on the more crowded isle of England, which he had imagined would return him to collective experience and public meaning. Marooned on his private island, he discovers the loneliness that in England he later senses had been there all along:

> The sun set in the sea; the same odd sun
> rose from the sea,
> and there was one of it and one of me.
> The island had one kind of everything:
> one tree snail,

and so on in a solitary's parody of Noah's ark. Bishop's repetition drums home the sound of desolation. The first line from this stanza begins and ends alliteratively in "the sun" he cannot get rid of; he even calls it "the same" sun. The words "From the sea" follow quickly after the similar words "in the sea." Then, with the same stagnant sound, comes the repetitive beat "one of . . . and one of," tapped to conclusion by the simple rhyme of the second and third lines (sea and me), and of the first line and its dominating word (sun) with the lonely and similarly dominating word of the third line (one).

Eventually, though, the loneliness gets interrupted.

> Just when I thought I couldn't stand it
> another minute longer, Friday came.
> (Accounts of that have everything all wrong.)
> Friday was nice.
> Friday was nice, and we were friends.
> If only he had been a woman!

Bishop's little joke about the work week comically suggests a real change; or, perhaps, the weekend reprieve only vents some pressure and then sends us right back to the weekday routine. Instead of sounding excited by his new companion, Crusoe sounds bored, using about the dullest verb and the tiredest adjective of praise he can find—"was nice"—and using them twice in a row, not with the emphasis his earlier repetitions imply, but instead with a Monday sound of defeated resignation at how inadequate a change Friday's arrival actually brought. He would prefer a woman. His desire, though (whether he realizes it or not), shifts a little to what's available, discreetly releasing a partly sexual curiosity: "Pretty to watch; he had a pretty body." Indeed, his admiration for Friday gives his resort to a bland expression like "was nice" a poignant hint of understated interest. Friday, he suspects, feels the same unspoken wondering, for when Crusoe says "I wanted to propagate my kind, / and so did he, I think," it sounds as if he slips into thinking (or projecting his own wish) that Friday wants to propagate not only his own kind, but also *Crusoe's* kind, wants to bear Crusoe's child.

The sexual uncertainty contributes to the general sense that Crusoe longs only for the places and people he does not have. Whatever happens, he can never feel happy. If he gets one thing, he wants the other. Alone on his island, he would "have given years, or taken a few, / for any sort of kettle," and he would shut his "eyes and think about a tree." In England, he has all that, but he thinks "I'm bored, too, drinking my real tea, / surrounded by uninteresting lumber." In the same way, when he had Friday's companionship, Friday was not the companion he wanted. When he returns to those he wanted, then he wants Friday. But then, as if to tease his pain, the people he returns to carry a disease that kills Friday. By that point he lives amidst the women he yearned for, but, though he does not say, he sounds too defeated to seek their company. He puts his disappointment in implicitly sexual terms. The "living soul" of his "knife," that once "reeked of meaning," now "has dribbled away." In past days, he says, "My blood was full of them [islands]; my brain / bred islands. But that archipelago / has petered out. I'm old." Metaphorically, he is "petered" out in the slangy sense—impotent.

His powerlessness has origins in a vaguely intricate anxiety that he takes out on a baby goat.

> One day I dyed a baby goat bright red
> with my red berries, just to see
> something a little different.
> And then his mother wouldn't recognize him.

Crusoe is not merely unable; he is unwilling. Somehow, the idea of parents and of babies, of begetting or bearing children, terrifies him, much as it terrifies or disturbs Bishop in "The Weed," "Filling Station," and so many other poems. Early in the poem, Crusoe reveals a particular interest in birth, for—in his own metaphor—the volcanic eruption of an "island being born" sets off his opening lines. Thus with his red berry dye he paints his own circumstances onto the baby goat, for his own mother would not recognize him after so many years apart, any more than Bishop's mother, who never saw her after age five, would recognize her. By reenacting his own separation on the goat, he enlarges his aloneness and shows it as something that he at least partly seeks. The safety of a painful but acknowledged separation can feel easier and less painful than the unpredictable traumas of a connection he cannot control.

He wants to look at his fear outside himself, then, for several apparently contradictory reasons: to eject it from himself, to put it where he can better see it and contemplate it, and, aggressively, he wants to extend himself, to make *more* of himself.

> But then I'd dream of things
> like slitting a baby's throat, mistaking it
> for a baby goat. I'd have
> nightmares of other islands
> stretching away from mine, infinities
> of islands, islands spawning islands,
> like frogs' eggs turning into polliwogs.

In these fantasies, is Crusoe the parent, or the child? As spawner, he seems the parent, and yet he also echoes or at least shows a kinship to the haunting panic, in Lowell's "After the Surprising Conversions," at a fantasized voice that groans " 'My friend, / Cut your own throat. Cut your own throat. Now! Now!' "[8] The dreamy displacements and transformations leap too wildly and perhaps too privately, too skillfully as defenses, for any clear or simple following or identifying. Crusoe takes a baby goat for a baby person, and thinks of killing it, and then imagines with horror giving birth to babies endlessly, uncontrollably, in a nightmare terror exactly consonant with the fear of childbirth in "The Weed." There, in "The Weed," plants invade the body. Here, animals do, squirmilly phallic frogs and tadpoles. Either way, the invader is definitively something *other*, something siphoned off into nightmare, because Crusoe and Bishop prefer to think of it as nothing like themselves, nothing that could turn and grow inside them and shiver the boundary of their fragile selfhood.

Probably nowhere, not even in "The Weed" or such dire laments as "Insomnia" and "Varick Street," does Bishop's selfhood expose its fragility so bluntly as in her major late poem, "In the Waiting Room." More often, she prefers indirection. In most poems, although she writes in first person, she doesn't get forthrightly personal. Crusoe, however, gets personal for her. When he says he'd "have / night- mares . . . / of islands, islands spawning islands"

> knowing that I had to live
> on each and every one, eventually,
> for ages, registering their flora,
> their fauna, their geography,

he envisions Bishop's life and brands it nightmare. She too has traveled from one land and island to another, registering in her poems, stories, and letters their life and landscape.[9] When she writes "Crusoe in England" she, like Crusoe, after many years in the south and away from her homeland, has returned to the north where she grew up (Boston), has lost someone from her faraway land whom she loved dearly, and, late in life, looks back over her past. It all makes an elaborate subterfuge, lighter and more comic in the guise of the fictional Crusoe than it probably would be in her own voice. But in "In the Waiting Room," she casts off such voices in favor of the subtler fiction of her recollected self, going even so far as to name herself in the poem: "you are an *Elizabeth*" (Bishop's italics), with an emphasis that proclaims her explosion of identity to be as startling a surprise to her as it might well have been to readers who had praised her restraint for almost forty years.

"In the Waiting Room" is full of surprise, and about surprise, apparently because the child is very confident that she knows who she is, and very wrong—both about who she is, and even more, perhaps, in the presumption she can know who she is. She starts out confidently, with the basic facts: "In Worcester, Massachusetts," she begins. And she continues in short, certain sentences: "It was winter. It got dark / early. The waiting room / was full of grown-up people. . . ." That focus on grown-ups, partly as if to differentiate them from her, and partly to identify with them as if she were grown-up too, starts to betray her uncertainty and expose an effort in her bare, short facts, a search for some desperately needed ground—though the strain shows more from hindsight, after we have read through the poem. In the meantime, she insists on her confidence, but, in the tones of a recovered childhood, it turns parenthetical: "(I could read)." The parentheses advertise what so far remains a merely tactical modesty; for such a mature little girl, reading is no great accomplishment, so that she pretends to drop in that information only to clarify the facts. But of course her point is that she has something to be modest about, because those same parentheses quietly call attention to her proud boast that she can do more than other children her age, and that therefore she is like an adult or even, since she exceeds expectations, better than adults, better even than her aunt Consuelo, whom she condescends to: "even then I knew she was / a foolish, timid woman."

Soon, however, the seams in her confidence show more clearly. Horrified at the sights in a *National Geographic*, she reads "it right straight through. / I was too shy to stop." Something is amiss here; usually, shyness would *make* someone stop. But the little girl fears that to stop in front of the other people in the waiting room would spotlight her as squeamishly unadult, and she badly wants to think of herself as more mature even than the aunt who watches over her.

The aunt provides a handy standard for comparison when something really startling happens. Frightened by the *National Geographic,* the young "Elizabeth" wants a reassurance as secure as the belief that all this takes place "In Worcester, Massachusetts." And so she "looked at the cover: / the yellow margins, the date" — and there ends the first stanza. What follows, though, shows how meager such reassurance is:

> Suddenly, from inside,
> came an *oh!* of pain
> — Aunt Consuelo's voice —
> not very loud or long.
> I wasn't at all surprised;
> even then I knew she was
> a foolish, timid woman.
> I might have been embarrassed,
> but wasn't. What took me
> completely by surprise
> was that it was *me:*
> my voice, in my mouth.
> Without thinking at all
> I was my foolish aunt,
> I — we — were falling, falling,
> our eyes glued to the cover
> of the *National Geographic,*
> February, 1918.
>
> I said to myself. three days
> and you'll be seven years old.
> I was saying it to stop
> the sensation of falling off
> the round, turning world
> into cold, blue-black space.

Here, certainty has toppled, has somehow popped free of physics, snapped the anchor of gravity and fallen, or floated off in a way

that she calls falling; for her repetition implies that the mere de-
notation of falling doesn't quite match the sensation she means to
describe. After all, she cannot "fall" off the world. Her not quite
literal choice of words marks her as stuck in the cultural habit that
moralizes disorientation and figures it as an elemental, even biblical
fall and expulsion—but not into any world she knows. Instead she
plummets into the unrecognizable universe of some bizarrely other
and moorless ontology, remarkably like the Man-Moth plummeting
from ahigh in the man's world without a moth's ability to fly, and
a little like the unbeliever suddenly cast on his principles, tumbling
from his precarious perch with no beliefs to cling to. It echoes also
Dickinson's conclusion to "I felt a Funeral, in my Brain,"

> And then a Plank in Reason, broke,
> And I dropped down, and down—
> And hit a World, at every plunge,
> And Finished knowing—then—[10]

with the seemingly endless permutations of interpretability Dickinson
launches by the double meanings of both "Finished" and "then"
("finished" can mean either stopped, or completed; "then" can mean
either then at that point, or *and* then at the next point). We cannot
tell where Dickinson is—at someone's funeral, at her own funeral,
in the grip of a headache or a migraine, in outer space or in inner
space, in a suspended moment or in all eternity. In the same way,
Bishop has completely lost the ability to know where she is, exactly
the opposite of her opening confidence that she sits in the waiting
room "In Worcester, Massachusetts."

Why lose her confidence exactly *then?* In a waiting room, we
often look at other people and feel them looking at us in a way that
provokes self-consciousness, as Bishop would surely have been made
to think from reading Flannery O'Connor's "Revelation," which
begins in an unforgettable waiting room that sets off an agony of
self-consciousness, a scene that would reverberate the more for Bishop
because it was published soon after O'Connor died and Bishop wrote
an article in memory of her, so that Bishop might well have paused
over how tragically familiar such a setting was to her fatally ill
friend.[11] Moreover, the young Bishop in the poem seems preoccupied
with the thought that her birthday is near, an event that typically
prompts self-conscious reflection about who and what we are.

But much of the point here is that the young girl doesn't know what arouses her sudden tumbling into vertigo. We can—and should—intimate a variety of causes, but if Bishop gave a straightforward explanation it would, in effect, orient the disorientation and take out the terror. She doesn't know where she is, but that startles her less than the recognition that she does know where her disorientation comes from. It comes, in what with brilliant gradualness turns into a brilliant pun, "from inside." Meaning, inside the dentist's office, or so Bishop at first leaves us to think; and maybe Aunt Consuelo, in the dentist's chair, really does scream. But, taking Bishop at her word that the "*oh!* of pain" speaks in "Aunt Consuelo's voice," the little girl discovers with astonishment that Aunt Consuelo's cry comes from inside her own girl's body, in her own voice and from her own mouth. She, who can read, seems accustomed to falling back on thought, unlike (or at least so she thinks) her "foolish aunt." But now, some renegade emotion from her body, her inside, usurps thought ("Without thinking at all") and makes her one with the aunt she had felt superior to, much as the volcanoes erupt in the magazine, and as the weed erupts from inside the similarly first-person speaker of "The Weed" and reasserts the odd independence of a bodily will, and much, also, as the horrible scream erupts from Bishop's mother in "In the Village," echoing in Bishop's ears for the rest of her life as a woeful reminder of her invisible link to a past that feels at once feminine, maternal, and beyond the control of will.

Somehow, this discovery of her internal, bodily, uncontrollable link to the feminine has to do not only with what she feels "from inside" herself but also with how those internal feelings erupt from the pictures inside the *National Geographic*. The magazine jars her by the analogy between volcanic eruption and the forces she feels gathering inside her; and the analogy also helps release those forces. Namely, it helps release her horrified and bewildered reaction to certain other sights in the magazine: cannibalism ("Long Pig"), ornamental mutilation, and female nudity. Of those three shocks, she saves female nudity for last, as if it is the most frightening to mention and the one she wants to mention most. It is the only one she returns to, and, of course, it is the center of a whole stream of mixed cultural and sexual voyeurism, of specially sanctioned sexual objectifying, that we associate with *National Geographic*, something Bishop would even have found before in poetry. In *Paterson*, William

Carlos Williams ogles women's breasts in a *National Geographic*. He sounds much more relaxed and appreciative than Bishop, and she and many other readers, especially women, might find his easy assumptions discomforting.[12]

The *National Geographic* thus strikes Bishop by its sudden opening to two strange old worlds: the radically foreign, and the radically but secretly feminine. Perhaps the foreign would not feel so unsettling if it were not intensified with the feminine, which unnerves the little girl by its blend of the unfamiliarly frank (nakedness) with the eerily familiar (the bodies that nakedness exposes). As she puzzles over the two urgings, she tries, not very successfully, to dissolve the feminine into the foreign. Apparently, the foreign feels safer. Even in its strangeness it feels more predictable, less cloaked in taboo; and it is, after all, what even a little child, hardly accustomed to the special permissions of *National Geographic*, might expect to find there.

> But I felt: you are an *I*,
> you are an *Elizabeth*,
> you are one of *them*.
> *Why* should you be one, too?

What does it make her if she is "one of *them*"? In a sense, her fear of some likeness with "those awful hanging breasts"—much more evocative than the knees, trousers, boots, hands, or voices—suggests that she fears an identification with women in particular. But against the threat she sees in those breasts, her mention of trousers and "anyone" reassures her by including both women and men in her references to knees, hands, "*them*," or "us all." It reassures her only by comparison, though, for the discovery of a likeness to the people pictured in the magazine and to people in general still comes as a bewildering upheaval to the provincial girl "In Worcester, Massachusetts" who feels superior because she reads and can condescend to her allegedly foolish aunt. Until this moment, she had thought that being a self, an "Elizabeth" (the formally proper name suggests something special) made her different from other people. Now she switches from that assertion of singularity ("you are an *Elizabeth*") to an opposite assertion of commonality ("you are one of *them*") in the very next line, without syntactical transition, and with, instead, all the abruptness of her convulsive realization. When she says then that she felt afraid "to see what it was I was," her phrasing—"was

I was"—perfectly enacts the reflexive circularity of ordinary identity, the dead end of self that, against all her haughty presumption, she feels suddenly and irrevocably caught up in. As she says in an earlier, prose recounting of the same moment: "I felt . . . *myself*. In a few days it would be my seventh birthday. I felt *I, I, I*."[13]

She had thought her aunt was foolish and timid, but now she herself is too timid to look up at other people and be reminded that they see her as like themselves. Yet she wants to look, she wants to see if they really are like her. And so, hesitantly, she gives "a sidelong glance" at "knees, / trousers and skirts and boots." She looks at them, but like Mrs. Turpin in "Revelation," she reassures herself by looking *down* at them, at their feet. Mrs. Turpin, like the young girl in Bishop's poem, suddenly in the waiting room feels staggered by the ordinariness of her identity, which—in the O'Connor comic idiom that delighted Bishop—Mrs. Turpin phrases by the agonized question, " 'How am I a hog?' "[14] With the same elemental befuddlement, Bishop asks "Why should I be my aunt, / or me, or anyone?" Why must she have what all at once seems the terrible burden of any identity at all? It did not seem a burden as long as she could imagine her identity was special. The *National Geographic* trades on an unwitting sense of specialness in western culture. Westerners look; others are looked at, and nakedly, as if absolutely (or so it can seem, to a westerner whose experience of other cultures comes through magazine pictures). But by making almost explicit the presumption in the way westerners often objectify other cultures, the magazine can also expose the contrivance behind that presumption. Underneath our veneer of clothing, we are like them. Bishop's poem thus critiques the notion of exotica that such magazines foster, the sense that other cultures are inherently strange and definitively other. It shows the little girl at the precise moment when she discovers something central both about what she is and about what she is not. She is not alone. She must give up her fantasized distinctiveness and recognize that she is like other people.

Especially, she is like other girls and women.

> What similarities—
>   .   .   .   .
> I felt in my throat, or even
> the *National Geographic*

> and those awful hanging breasts—
> held us all together
> or made us all just one?

Those breasts represent not only other women but also what her own breasts will or might become. It is harder for her to think about bodies than to think about minds, for in her precociousness she can more easily sustain the illusion that she—the girl who can read and who sees foolishness in the adults around her—has mastered the world of mind.

A more searching analogy than "Revelation," therefore, is to O'Connor's "A Temple of the Holy Ghost," where an older but still prepubescent girl floats into reverie at the not quite dawning realization of her body's feminine distinctiveness. To keep from thinking about her body, she clings to the refuge of her precocious intellect. But the taboos are strong against literary contemplation of the feminine body as anything but a masculine object. O'Connor, in her letters, insists that the story is about the Eucharist,[15] and at the end she foists on a layer of Eucharistic symbology as if it were the point all along, when it seems instead that, from the beginning, the talk of the Holy Ghost is more a brilliant evasion of what rests most strongly on the various characters' minds, namely: their developing bodies, the difference between men's bodies and women's bodies, and sex and reproduction. When, by the end, the imagery of body blends with imagery of the Eucharist, it suggests that the Eucharist has become a vehicle for wonderings about the feminine body and blood, about maturation and menstruation. The young girl in O'Connor's story chafes at her sense of emerging likeness to her boy-crazy cousins, and starts to wonder, through the deflection of some talk about rabbits, how babies are born. Similarly, the little girl in Bishop's poem chafes at her sense of emerging likeness to grown women, and asks "How had I come to be here, / like them," wondering about the bodily origins of her own body, that is, about where babies come from, and about how those origins connect her to the bodies of other women all around her.

But the anxieties of fictional girls and women are expected to center on men, money, or religion, not on themselves. Boys and men are allowed and expected, in, say, Hemingway's stories or Fitzgerald's *The Great Gatsby* or Faulkner's *Light in August*, to agonize over their own sexual identity as well as over girls and women. As poignantly as any characters in American literature, O'Connor's characters agonize over their sexuality, but outside her stories she does not feel at liberty to acknowledge that universal trauma. In the same way, sexual identity is an almost secret subject of a great many Bishop poems. And yet, except perhaps in "Roosters," it oddly remains secret until "In the Waiting Room." Somehow she obscures her preoccupation with sexual identity even when it explodes forth, as in "The Weed," or when she pries into it, as in "Gwendolyn," the story where she and her cousin Billy unwrap from its tissue paper the very special doll that reminds them so much of her dead friend. "We handled her carefully. We took off her hat and shoes and stockings, and examined every stitch of her underclothes. Then we played vaguely at 'operating' on her stomach."[16]

Bishop repeatedly wants to explore interiors, whether of dolls or people, filling stations or geography. As far back as an editorial for her high school magazine, she insists on the primacy of what lies inside, using metaphors that would erupt again when she wrote "In the Waiting Room" so many years later:

> How very boring the world would be were it not for the rebellious and uncontrolled lava within it that does queer and violent things whenever it feels like it. . . . We have in ourselves, not the boiling lava of the earth, but a kind of burning, unceasing energy of some sort that will not let us be finished off and live in the world like the china people on the mantlepiece. This energy, this fire, is always there, ready to explode or to burn fretfully, to show itself surprisingly in our work, our games, our looks and actions. It is the part of us that the *Blue Pencil* [her magazine] uses for its stories and poems—and editorials.[17]

That same curiosity about the interior and its link to her imagination continues throughout her publishing career, from, at the beginning, "The Weed" and "The Fish" (with its "coarse white flesh / packed in like feathers," its "shiny entrails" and "pink swim-bladder"), through "Gwendolyn" and "Filling Station" and "In the Waiting Room." While—as she says in "Gwendolyn"—she always handles things ever so carefully, Bishop wants to know just what hides inside and underneath, especially inside and underneath women's bodies, whether because of her emerging homoerotic curiosity, or, more fully in "In the Waiting Room," because she wants to know what latent power hides inside her own body, ready to sprout forth suddenly like a dreamed-up weed, or to grow gradually like a girl's breasts.

All this tells us not only about what Bishop does in "In the Waiting Room," but also, perhaps, why it took her so many years to do it. It might put things too strongly to say that the distinctiveness of feminine anatomy as a poetic subject, as opposed to a masculine object, was not allowed. For its potential as a subject was not even recognized enough to be explicitly forbidden. But Bishop lived into a time of changing and enlarging standards. Rather poignantly, not until her last completed poem, "Sonnet," ending with an exclamation point and a newly redefined word—"gay!"—does she complete a poem of explicit homosexuality. The changes in standards helped her write and think in ways she could not write or think in before. Late in life she recovers the lyric sexuality that most other writers, as heterosexuals, agonize over in their youth.

She first wrote about the incident described in "In the Waiting Room" in a prose piece from about 1961;[18] but in that version the shock of identity is all abstract and universal and has nothing to do with bodies or with matters feminine. Indeed, much as the change in her writing has to do with changes in the world around her, it is intensely personal as well. Her best prose, stories like "In the Village" and "Gwendolyn," turns to retrospect twenty years before she finishes any major poems in the same mode. In the early 1950s, when she settled happily in Brazil, the country setting reminded her of Nova Scotia and made her feel comfortable writing about her childhood.[19] *Where* she was, then, seems to have mattered most to what she wrote. In her poems, she wrote about place, just as she fascinated friends with descriptions of Brazil in her letters, and even wrote the Time-Life book on Brazil. Still, she confined her retrospective meditations to prose, except in "Manners," a thoroughly pleasant but not very searching or personal poem, and "First Death in Nova Scotia," which has much more of the later poems' retrospective rumination. Both "First Death in Nova Scotia" and "In the Waiting Room" begin with place: "In Worcester, Massachusetts" and "In the cold, cold parlor." In the later poem, though, place turns out to be an evasion, to be beside the point, as the real action occurs inside the girl, not inside the dentist's office. By contrast, in the earlier poem, place—the coldness of the parlor and the people in it, and the coldness outside that sets a boundary for where the dead

can go—largely turns out to be the point. For some private reason
or reasons, she saved the poetry of retrospect for later. Even "The
Moose," as we have seen, she began thinking about in 1946, but
could not complete until 1972.

Probably, the change has to do simply with aging and the way it
makes us look back on our accumulated losses, as Bishop does in
"One Art." Such feelings would be encouraged by the changes in
her life that made her losses sting: the illness and suicide of Lota
de Macedo Soares, Bishop's companion of many years in Brazil, and
Bishop's consequent decision to leave Brazil and her homes there
(referred to in "One Art") that meant so much to her. The feeling
of change bewildered Bishop when she returned to the states,[20] and
the expanding discussion of feminism that she would have found
seems to make a difference to her poetry.

A crucial line in "The Moose" has much to do with the feminine
solidarity of "In the Waiting Room." After a perhaps kindly but
certainly foolish "man's voice assures us / 'Perfectly harmless . . . ,' "
as if he supposes that people, women especially, fear the moose might
ram the bus to destruction like some bull-moose Moby-Dick, someone
whispers with astonishment a line that could make an epigraph to
"The Moose" and "In the Waiting Room" together: " 'Look! It's a
she!' " Somehow, the world of masculine standards has made the
very fact of she-ness a surprise. "How," thinks the girl in the waiting
room, "—I didn't know any / word for it—how 'unlikely'. . ."
(Bishop's ellipsis). She cannot fathom "What similarities . . . / held
us all together / or made us all just one." Her point, though, is that
people in general and women in particular are indeed just one.

Of course, that cannot in every respect be true. She could as well
draw attention to the differences among people—something that
Bishop the traveler was thoroughly familiar with and often called
attention to. Here, though, she holds up for criticism the western
presumption of natural privilege, and, more intimately, the egotism
of our private wish to imagine that our individual selves are in some
pure way more privileged than the other selves around us. On the
contrary, in the waiting room, Bishop discovers that men, and women,
right down to their bodies, are perfectly common, and, implicitly,
she celebrates that commonness.

But, at least while she is a precocious six- (almost seven!) year-
old, she has no vocabulary for it. How "unlikely." The bare exis-

tentialism of identity exceeds the reach of her language. The limit
of the lexicon, culturally as well as linguistically, has deepened her
discovery of something thoroughly ordinary until it is also a discovery
of something all profound. Still, the circumstances of her discovery
suggest a loss that offers a language for her gain. As in "The Moose"
and "Crusoe in England," the approach of endings provokes a meditation over beginnings. Late in her life, Bishop recalls how the
anxiousness over her nearing seventh birthday made her think about
universal things. Birthdays, along with their pleasures, have a way
of making us think about death days. And death, Bishop reminds
us, was in the air: "The War was on."[21] She has felt a new profundity
sprout up within her, but outside, things are as they were before,
mired in "night and slush and cold, / and it was still the fifth / of
February, 1918." The new profundity can change her, but it cannot
save her from what sweeps the world around her. It is, after all, a
realization of her common susceptibility to everything around her,
including death, the ultimate metaphor of our common humanity.
Late in life, after a spree of wish and a settling into place, Bishop
looks back in retrospect to her childhood, and from that vantage,
also looks forward to find that we all sit in the waiting room.

Notes

All references to Bishop's poems and translations of poetry are to Elizabeth Bishop, *The Complete Poems: 1927-1979* (New York: Farrar, Straus & Giroux, 1983). For the dates of Bishop's publications, along with much other bibliographical information, see Candace W. MacMahon, *Elizabeth Bishop: A Bibliography, 1927-1979* (Charlottesville: University Press of Virginia, 1980), or Diana E. Wyllie, *Elizabeth Bishop and Howard Nemerov: A Reference Guide* (Boston: G. K. Hall, 1983).

Chapter One

1. Boswell's *Life of Johnson*, ed. George Birkbeck Hill and L. F. Powell (Oxford: Oxford University Press, 1934), I: 471.

2. *The Poems of Emily Dickinson*, ed. Martha Dickinson Bianchi and Alfred Leete Hampson (Boston: Little, Brown, 1930), 218. All quotations from Dickinson in this chapter come from this edition, the sort Bishop might have read in the years before writing "The Weed," though I do not insist on any necessarily conscious or absolute influence. For convenience, I also refer to the poems by their numbers in the now standard and sometimes much different edition, *The Poems of Emily Dickinson*, ed. Thomas H. Johnson (Cambridge: Harvard University Press, 1955), where this is poem 445. Late in life Bishop said that at age twelve "I had read Emily Dickinson, but an early edition, and I didn't like it much"; George Starbuck, " 'The Work!': A Conversation with Elizabeth Bishop," in *Elizabeth Bishop and Her Art*, ed. Lloyd Schwartz and Sybil P. Estes (Ann

Arbor: University of Michigan Press, 1983), 319. We cannot know whether to take Bishop's early dislike of Dickinson—or memory or claim of disliking Dickinson—as casual fact or as motivated denial. A letter Bishop wrote to Anne Stevenson confirms the implication that she read the 1955 edition and liked it more (letter of Jan. 8, 1964, in the Elizabeth Bishop Papers, Washington University Libraries, St. Louis, Missouri). Indeed, among the materials now housed in the Elizabeth Bishop Collection, Rare Books and Manuscripts, Vassar College Library, Poughkeepsie, New York (hereafter referred to as Vassar College Library), Bishop left some notes for a "Dickinson/Hopkins poem"; and before 1955 she reviewed both a collection of Dickinson's letters and a book on Dickinson. Of the letters she observed that, "As in her poetry, Emily Dickinson is interested in Geography (in which "Heaven" seems to be one of the most familiar places)." The comment shows Bishop taking special note of Dickinson's writing on an afterlife, and shows her strongly relating Dickinson to her own preoccupation with geography. *The New Republic* 125 (Aug. 27, 1951): 20. For the other review see *The New Republic* 127 (Aug. 18, 1952): 20. See also Lynn Keller and Cristanne Miller, "Emily Dickinson, Elizabeth Bishop, and the Rewards of Indirection," *New England Quarterly* 57 (1984): 533-53 (the unpublished review Keller and Miller refer to [p. 535n, relying on another scholar's error] is in fact the 1952 review published in *The New Republic*).

3. The line derives from George Herbert's "Love-unknowne," "Each day, each hour, each moment of the week" (line 69), a poem Bishop cited as a source for "The Weed" in Ashley Brown, "An Interview with Elizabeth Bishop," in Schwartz and Estes, eds., 294-95; and in a talk published as "Elizabeth Bishop: Influences," *The American Poetry Review* 14 (Jan./Feb., 1985): 11-14.

4. For a wide-ranging speculation on anxieties about creativity that have specifically or disproportionately burdened women, see Sandra M. Gilbert and Susan Gubar, *The Madwoman in the Attic: The Woman Writer and the Nineteenth-Century Literary Imagination* (New Haven: Yale University Press, 1979), 45-92. Alicia Suskin Ostriker, *Stealing the Language: The Emergence of Women's Poetry in America* (Boston: Beacon Press, 1986), 1-58, reviews similar issues in the particular context of American women's poetry.

5. Quoted in Bonnie Costello, "Marianne Moore and Elizabeth Bishop: Friendship and Influence," *Twentieth Century Literature* 30 (1984): 140; see also 135.

6. Vassar College Library.

7. On daemonic possession, see Angus Fletcher, *Allegory: The Theory of a Symbolic Mode* (Ithaca, N.Y.: Cornell University Press, 1964), 25-69.

8. M. H. Abrams, *The Mirror and the Lamp: Romantic Theory and the Critical Tradition* (Oxford: Oxford University Press, 1953), 156-225.

9. See the interview with Brown, and Bishop's remarks in *The American Poetry Review.* In both cases she refers to Coleridge's discussion of Herbert in the *Biographia Literaria,* chapter 19, where he also quotes other Herbert poems ("Virtue," "The Bosom Sin") that seem to suggest imagery for "The Weed." Some years later, when Bishop's friend May Swenson wrote that she was reading the *Biographia* and assembling a set of notes on it, Bishop wrote back: "*Biographia Literaria* is one of the best books I know for 'ideas' — and do please send me your notes [on it] — it is filled with wonderful things," and added that she had quoted it in "The Sea & Its Shore," one of her early stories; letter of Feb. 10, 1954, in the May Swenson Papers, Washington University Libraries, St. Louis, Missouri. In "The Sea & Its Shore," the passage about anti-mnemonics (Elizabeth Bishop, *The Collected Prose,* ed. Robert Giroux [New York: Farrar, Straus & Giroux, 1984], 176) comes from chapter 3 of the *Biographia,* ed. James Engell and W. Jackson Bate (Princeton, N.J.: Princeton University Press, 1983), I: 49 and n. (Bishop, of course, would have read an earlier edition.)

10. Abrams himself denies that he uses any deliberate method. See his remarks quoted in Wayne C. Booth, "History as Metaphor: Or, Is M. H. Abrams a Mirror, or a Lamp, or a Fountain, or...?" in *High Romantic Argument: Essays for M. H. Abrams,* ed. Lawrence Lipking (Ithaca, N.Y.: Cornell University Press, 1981), 92. For other challenges to Abrams's objectivity, see J. Hillis Miller, "Tradition and Difference," *Diacritics* 2 (Winter, 1972), 6-13; Booth; and Lawrence Lipking, "The Genie in the Lamp: M. H. Abrams and the Motives of Literary History," in Lipking, ed., 79-105 and 128-48. For other observations that Abrams proceeds like a mirror, see Miller, 10; Booth; and Jonathan Culler, "The Mirror Stage," in Lipking, ed., 157.

11. Abrams, esp. 203 and 210.

12. Abrams, 173-74.

13. Samuel Taylor Coleridge, *Shakespearean Criticism,* ed. Thomas Middleton Raysor, 2nd ed. (London: J. M. Dent, 1960), I: 198; Abrams, 224. I do not claim Coleridge's term as a source for Bishop, though it would be rash to rule it out as one of innumerable, possible, and partial sources.

14. Walter Pater complains that Coleridge implies such a loss. Pater sees it more as an inert submission to some naturally mechanical process than

as a threat. That leads Abrams to dispense with Pater's criticism as mistaken, for Coleridge's idea is anything but passive and mechanical: Pater, *Appreciations, with an Essay on Style* (1889; reprint, London: Macmillan, 1910), 80-81; Abrams, 224. The question of how much or little credence Coleridge gave to unconscious imagination is rather vexed. James Volant Baker, *The Sacred River: Coleridge's Theory of the Imagination* (Baton Rouge: Louisiana State University Press, 1957), 175-76 and 184-85, suggests that Coleridge gave it more weight some years after the 1808 lecture on Shakespeare that Abrams and I note gives it so little weight. See also Humphry House, *Coleridge* (1953; reprint, London: Rupert Hart-Davis, 1967), 145-56.

15. Nathaniel Hawthorne, *The Scarlet Letter* (Columbus: Ohio State University Press, 1962), 131 (Ch. X).

16. The idea of organic art as unified art is implicit throughout Abrams's discussion, and at times he addresses it directly, such as pp. 174-75, 204, and 220-22. Although Abrams's historical emphasis pits him against the New Critical hegemony then rising around him, his insistence on organicism reveals a bond with those he implicitly criticizes. More recently, he has written an insightful critique of the current doubt that art or criticism can be unified: "The Deconstructive Angel," *Critical Inquiry* 3 (1977): 425-38.

17. Quoted in David Kalstone, "Trial Balances: Elizabeth Bishop and Marianne Moore," in *Coming to Light: American Women Poets in the Twentieth Century*, ed. Diane Wood Middlebrook and Marilyn Yalom (Ann Arbor: University of Michigan Press, 1985), 120.

18. Ellen Moers, *Literary Women* (Garden City, N.Y.: Doubleday, 1976), 90-99, notes the connection between Mary Shelley's frequent and uneasy pregnancies and the plot of *Frankenstein*.

19. Mary Shelley, *Frankenstein or The Modern Prometheus* (1831; reprint, London: Oxford University Press, 1969), 88, 93 (Ch. 8), 217, 222 (Ch. 24).

20. *Frankenstein*, 8-9.

21. *Shelley's Prose and Poetry*, ed. Donald H. Reiman and Sharon B. Powers (New York: W. W. Norton, 1977), 504. Similarly, he says that "Poetry . . . is not subject to the controul of the active powers of the mind, and that its *birth* and recurrence has no necessary connexion with consciousness or will" (italics added), 506.

22. And, as Abrams notes in *The Mirror and the Lamp*, 213-17, like Blake, Wordsworth, Hazlitt, Keats, Carlyle, and others.

23. We need no testimony to such pleasure, but happen to have some. Bishop confessed her "conceit" about "The Weed" to Marianne Moore,

who had taken an interest in the poem. See Candace W. MacMahon, *Elizabeth Bishop: A Bibliography, 1927-1979* (Charlottesville: University Press of Virginia, 1980), 142-43.

24. *Leaves of Grass,* ed. Harold W. Blodgett and Sculley Bradley (New York: New York University Press, 1965), 113-14. Bishop named Whitman as a poet she especially favored in her adolescence: letter of Jan. 8, 1964, to Anne Stevenson in the Elizabeth Bishop Papers, Washington University Libraries; Ashley Brown, "An Interview with Elizabeth Bishop," 292. In the typescript of an unpublished talk, she uses Whitman to represent "one's idea of a US poet" in "Three American Poets," Vassar College Library.

25. Compare "Love-unknowne":

> . . . I hasted to my bed
> But when I thought to sleep out all the faults
> (I sigh to speak)
> I found that some had stuff'd the bed with thoughts,
> I would say *thorns.* Deare, could my heart not break,
> When with my pleasure ev'n my rest was gone?

These lines make a close model for Bishop's poem, with Herbert's thorns transformed to her weed.

26. Lionel Trilling, "A Speech on Robert Frost: A Cultural Episode," *Partisan Review* 26 (Summer, 1959): 445-52, reprinted in *Robert Frost: A Collection of Critical Essays,* ed. James M. Cox (Englewood Cliffs, N.J.: Prentice-Hall, 1962), 151-58. Just as some readers, before Trilling, saw a more complicated Frost, so other critics besides myself have begun to suggest a more complicated Bishop. David Kalstone says that "Merely to praise her 'famous eye' would be a way of avoiding larger issues. We need to know what is seen, and how the eye . . . initiates us into human fears and wishes." "Questions of Memory, Questions of Travel," in Schwartz and Estes, eds., 4. Kalstone's helpful essay concentrates more on the what and the how; my own discussion tries to probe as much into the fears and wishes. Helen Vendler similarly insists on the uneasier side of Bishop's poetry where, especially in the later and sometimes more explicit poems, she finds a "vibration . . . between two frequencies—the domestic and the strange," and a "guerilla attack of the alien, springing from the very bulwarks of the familiar." "Domestication, Domesticity, and the Other-worldly," in Schwartz and Estes, eds., 32, 37. Denis Donoghue, *Connoisseurs of Chaos: Ideas of Order in Modern American Poetry,* 2nd ed. (New York: Columbia University Press, 1984), 246-81, draws as much attention to

Bishop's sense of panic as to her composure. Patricia B. Wallace, in a recent general overview, observes as I do that Bishop has been read too exclusively as restrained and tame. "The Wildness of Elizabeth Bishop," *Sewanee Review* 19 (1985): 95-115. At the same time, just when some critics have begun to take Bishop more complicatedly, the outspokenness of much recent women's poetry can tempt us to relegate her back to the land of the timid. Among commentators who celebrate the boldness of more recent women poets, at least two stand out for their balanced recognition that Bishop, in her quieter way, shares much with the more explosive poets who follow her: see Adrienne Rich, "The Eye of the Outsider: The Poetry of Elizabeth Bishop," *Boston Review* 8 (April, 1983): 15-17, and Ostriker.

27. Incidentally, this never seems to have occurred to Bishop, if we can take at face value her comments in an interview published over twenty years after the poem. Upon being told that "Filling Station" was cited as a feminist exemplar, she said, "But no woman appears in it at all." When her interviewer refers then to the evidence of a woman, she interrupts: "I never . . . Isn't it strange? I certainly didn't feel sorry for whoever crocheted that thing! Isn't that strange!" George Starbuck, " 'The Work!': A Conversation with Elizabeth Bishop," in Schwartz and Estes, eds., 321. Bishop observes that a feminist reading is strange to her, that is, perhaps, unfamiliar. She does not say she finds it wrong, though elsewhere in the interview she often speaks out strongly. Feeling sorry is not necessarily an issue. The unseen woman could be as happy as anyone ever is. But the signs of her still imply circumstances that Bishop, knowingly or not, has left us able to describe, and that some of us may not prefer. It may be worth adding that many of Bishop's comments about her own past or her ideas are oddly inconsistent with each other or with verifiable fact, such as her comment that after writing "In the Waiting Room," which is supposedly based on her memory of the February, 1918, *National Geographic*, she "checked it out in the New York Public Library" (the extra detail gives a sound of authority) and found that the "African things, it turned out, were in the *next* issue, in March" (Starbuck, 318). They are not in either issue. (See Ch. 4.)

28. Robert Lowell misses this central tactic in his poetic rendering of Bishop's story "The Scream" (derived from Elizabeth Bishop's story "In the Village") in *For the Union Dead* (New York: Farrar, Straus & Giroux, 1964), 8-9, where he has Bishop refer to her mother as "Mother" and "my mother."

29. Clarice Lispector, "The Smallest Woman in the World," *Kenyon*

Review 26 (1964): 501-6; Elizabeth Bishop and the Editors of *Life, Brazil* (New York: Time, 1962); letter of Oct. 10, 1951, to May Swenson in the May Swenson Papers, Washington University Libraries.

Chapter Two

1. *Occasion* refers to the event or context that calls forth a poem. Every poem has an occasion, though few give their occasions special attention. When they do, we call them occasional poems—poems written in honor of or response to particular, often public events, such as Oliver Wendell Holmes's "Old Ironsides" (responding to an announcement that the famous ship would be destroyed), Tennyson's "Ode on the Death of the Duke of Wellington," Yeats's "Easter, 1916" (on the Easter Rebellion in Ireland), or Auden's "September 1, 1939" (on the start of World War II).

2. Harold Bloom's brief comments on "The Unbeliever" have much aided the following discussion; Bloom, Foreword, in *Elizabeth Bishop and Her Art*, ed. Lloyd Schwartz and Sybil P. Estes (Ann Arbor: University of Michigan Press, 1983), x.

3. Characteristically, both in her poems and apparently in her daily life, Bishop enjoyed looking across the landscape from above. For anecdotal, biographical examples, see Ashley Brown, "Elizabeth Bishop in Brazil," in Schwartz and Estes, eds., 223-26; and Mildred J. Nash, "Elizabeth Bishop's Library: A Reminiscence," *Massachusetts Review* 24 (1983): 434. The watercolor sketch reproduced on the cover of the *The Complete Poems: 1927-1979* nicely illustrates this habit of perspective, and Bishop often refers to her view of the landscape—or her binoculars—in her letters.

4. Dickinson, poem 1712, in *The Poems of Emily Dickinson*, ed. Thomas H. Johnson (Cambridge: Harvard University Press, 1955). R. W. Franklin is probably right to see this text of the poem as incomplete, though because his suggested additions would not affect the comparison with Bishop, I have given the text as it is most commonly available. See R. W. Franklin, "The Houghton Library Dickinson Manuscript 157," *Harvard Library Bulletin* 27 (1980): 245-57.

5. John Bunyan, *The Pilgrim's Progress*, ed. James Blanton Wharey (London: Oxford University Press, 1928), 41. Bunyan, in turn, is quoting Proverbs 23.34. Bishop takes a number of details from this scene in *The Pilgrim's Progress*, but her allegory differs freely from Bunyan's.

6. Bishop began her sexual activity heterosexually and later turned to homosexuality. Published comments are usually discreet. For the most de-

tailed, see "The Art of Poetry XXVII: Elizabeth Bishop," *The Paris Review* 80 (1981): 75-76; Ian Hamilton, *Robert Lowell: A Biography* (New York: Random House, 1982), 135. Curiously, even late in life she could refer to marriage a little wistfully: "It never worked for me, but I don't regret — all things considered — it's not happening," quoted in Nash, 435. In an apparently spur-of-the-moment gesture in 1975, Bishop drew as her entire self-portrait a left hand with a bright ring — not clearly a wedding ring, but still where a wedding ring might go — and then labeled the ring "Imaginary"; *Self-Portrait: Book People Picture Themselves,* from the collection of Burt Britton (New York: Random House, 1976), 84.

7. See Jonathan Culler, *Structuralist Poetics: Structuralism, Linguistics, and the Study of Literature* (Ithaca, N.Y.: Cornell University Press, 1975), 131-60, 260-62; Robert Dale Parker, *Faulkner and the Novelistic Imagination* (Urbana: University of Illinois Press, 1985), 31-38.

8. The fallacy of imitative form is the idea that merely by making the form imitate the content you can make admirable art. Of course, we often appreciate imitative form, but in itself that cannot make good art and there is a boundary to its artistic value. Otherwise someone could write well about chaos or confusion simply by producing a chaotic or confused text — a boundary that Modernist and Postmodernist literature sometimes presses.

9. T. S. Eliot, *The Complete Poems and Plays: 1909-1950* (New York: Harcourt, Brace, Jovanovich, 1971), 48, lines 360-66.

10. Norma Procopiow, "Survival Kit: The Poetry of Elizabeth Bishop," *Centennial Review* 25 (1981): 1-19. Bishop's whole life, more than most people's, was made of traumatic splits, regardless of any relation someone might presume those traumas had to her eventual sexual changes or preferences. She was split early from her father, then from her mother, then the return of her mother seems (as recounted in "In the Village") to have forecast a split from the grandparents she'd gone to when she first split from her mother. Then of course she soon split from her mother all over again, and then from one set of grandparents to another, and then from them to boarding school and back to both sets of grandparents and to an aunt — all this taking her only up to about the age of seven.

11. *The Poems of Tennyson,* ed. Christopher Ricks (London: Longman, 1969), 357-58, lines 62, 71-72.

12. Anne Stevenson, *Elizabeth Bishop* (New York: Twayne, 1966), 65.

13. On the visionary implications of the star simile see Lloyd Schwartz, "The Mechanical Horse and the Indian Princess: Two Poems from *North & South,*" *World Literature Today* 51 (1977): 42.

14. For example, in *Lion in the Garden: Interviews with William Faulkner, 1926-1962*, ed. James B. Meriwether and Michael Millgate (New York: Random House, 1968), 88-89.

15. Denis Donoghue feels a similar strain at the ending, and Bishop wrote him to protest his sense that it calls for so much attention; *Connoisseurs of Chaos: Ideas of Order in Modern American Poetry*, 2nd ed. (New York: Columbia University Press, 1984), 269-70. On the other hand, Mary J. Elkins, "Elizabeth Bishop and the Art of Seeing," *South Atlantic Review* 48 (1983): 51, argues against my view here that the ending is marred by an easy sentimentality.

16. Procopiow, p. 9, similarly finds the politics of "A Miracle for Breakfast" unconvincing. Bishop's letters to Marianne Moore show her own uneasiness about the sestina form: "the sestina is just a sort of stunt." See Candace W. MacMahon, *Elizabeth Bishop: A Bibliography, 1927-1979* (Charlottesville: University Press of Virginia, 1980), 143-44.

17. Penelope Laurans, " 'Old Correspondences': Prosodic Transformations in Elizabeth Bishop," in Schwartz and Estes, eds., 84-85.

18. MacMahon, p. 146, notes that in its first publication "Late Air" was signed *"Key West."*

19. Elizabeth Bishop, *The Collected Prose*, ed. Robert Giroux (New York: Farrar, Straus & Giroux, 1984), 172. Subsequent references to this edition in this chapter will appear in text.

20. Bulmer is pronounced, and sometimes spelled, as Boomer, according to Robert Giroux, Introduction to Bishop, *The Collected Prose*, xx, and Peter Sanger, "Elizabeth Bishop and Nova Scotia," *Antigonish Review* 60 (1985): 27.

21. Giroux dates it as "probably" from 1966, p. 268.

22. MacMahon, 145.

23. *Leaves of Grass*, ed. Harold W. Blodgett and Sculley Bradley (New York: New York University Press, 1965), 254.

24. Helen Vendler mentions a likeness between Bishop and Whitman in reference to Bishop's uncharacteristically overt, late poem of recollected crisis, "In the Waiting Room," in "Domestication, Domesticity, and the Otherworldly," Schwartz and Estes, eds., 37-38.

25. Nina Baym, "Melodramas of Beset Manhood: How Theories of American Fiction Exclude Women Authors," *American Quarterly* 33 (1981): 123-39, reprinted in *The New Feminist Criticism: Essays on Women, Literature, and Theory*, ed. Elaine Showalter (New York: Pantheon, 1985), 63-80. Some readers, however, have always been taken in by Whitman's celebrations of

self and country in other poems, so that they see only the optimistic Poet of Democracy and overlook the considerable extent to which Whitman yawps out his confidence in defense against his ever-returning doubts.

26. Wallace Stevens, *Collected Poems* (New York: Knopf, 1954), 130.

Chapter Three

1. Barbara Page, "Shifting Islands: Elizabeth Bishop's Manuscripts," *Shenandoah* 33, no. 1 (1981-82): 55-56, shows that Bishop deliberately worked out the phrasing of this line through many revisions.

2. See the autobiographical short story "In the Village" and the prose memoir "The Country Mouse" in Elizabeth Bishop, *The Collected Prose*, ed. Robert Giroux (New York: Farrar, Straus & Giroux, 1984).

3. David Kalstone, "Elizabeth Bishop: Questions of Memory, Questions of Travel," in *Elizabeth Bishop and Her Art*, ed. Lloyd Schwartz and Sybil P. Estes (Ann Arbor: University of Michigan Press, 1983), 11.

4. "The 'Darwin' Letter," in Schwartz and Estes, eds., p. 288. "My own favorite reading is Darwin," quoted in Wesley Wehr, "Elizabeth Bishop: Conversations and Class Notes," *Antioch Review* 39 (1981): 325.

5. For example, Anne Stevenson, *Elizabeth Bishop* (New York: Twayne, 1966), 96. Stevenson's disapproval is thoughtful and respectful.

6. Bishop told an interviewer, speaking of "Insomnia," "I never liked that. I almost left it out." "The Art of Poetry XXVII" in *The Paris Review* 80 (1981): 69. Candace W. MacMahon, *Elizabeth Bishop: A Bibliography, 1927-1979* (Charlottesville: University Press of Virginia, 1980), 16, quotes a letter from Bishop's publisher to the effect that Bishop "had some doubts" about "Insomnia."

7. See Alan Williamson, "*A Cold Spring*: The Poet of Feeling," in Schwartz and Estes, eds., 96-108, for a similar and in many respects corroborating reading, and a thoughtful comparison to other love poems in *A Cold Spring*.

8. See Jane Shore, "Elizabeth Bishop: The Art of Changing Your Mind," *Ploughshares* 5 (1979): 178-91.

9. Kenneth Clark, *Landscape into Art* (John Murray: London, 1949), Ch. 1, "The Landscape of Symbols," 1-15. Clark refers to "embroidered nature" on p. 9 and goes on to discuss landscape tapestries in the following pages, though I cannot find the specific phrase "tapestried landscape."

10. Annette Kolodny, *The Lay of the Land: Metaphor as Experience and History in American Life and Letters* (Chapel Hill: University of North

Carolina Press, 1975), explores the metaphorical rape of landscape in male American literature.

11. Margaret Homans, *Women Writers and Poetic Identity: Dorothy Wordsworth, Emily Brontë, and Emily Dickinson* (Princeton, N.J.: Princeton University Press, 1980), 12-40.

12. Adrienne Rich insightfully discusses ironic perspective in "Manuelzinho," noting how Bishop's epigraph carefully distances her (*"A friend of the writer is speaking"*) from the patronizing sympathies of her speaker. Compared to the gradually encroaching irony of "Brazil, January 1, 1502," however, the irony of "Manuelzinho" strikes me as heavy-handed, as almost as patronizing of the speaker as the speaker is of Manuelzinho. Rich aptly compares "Manuelzinho" to "Faustina, or Rock Roses," where, more as in "January 1," the speaker feels the sting of her own irony, which seems to me to make "Faustina" much more subtly ironic than "Manuelzinho." Adrienne Rich, "The Eye of the Outsider: The Poetry of Elizabeth Bishop," *Boston Review* 8 (April 1983): 17.

13. I hope I can say that about the European explorers without presuming something entirely superior in our own culture's partly more tolerant ways, ways that give me the perspective to make such a claim. In some respects, we do as the explorers did, in that culture is *our* commodity. Compare the discussion earlier in this chapter of Bishop's questioning her own motives for travel in "Questions of Travel."

14. Vespucci describes Indian culture with genuine interest. Without in the least romanticizing the Indians, he uses what he sees in Brazil to reinterpret some sacred tenets of his own culture. He himself was Italian, though on this particular voyage he was sponsored by the Portuguese. Nevertheless, it is tempting to note, given that all the New World soon took Amerigo Vespucci's name, that Bishop's poem describes not only the Brazilian encounter between Portuguese and Indians, but also the whole encounter between Old and New Worlds that can represent the formation of all America—North, South, and the ever-metaphorical America of the world's hopes and tragic failures to live up to those hopes. See (to name the major English-language source that Bishop at least *could* have seen, though she probably relied on materials in Portuguese) Frederick J. Pohl, *Amerigo Vespucci: Pilot Major* (New York: Columbia University Press, 1944), esp. 132-35.

15. "Brazil, January 1, 1502" was first published in the *New Yorker,* Jan. 2, 1960. Elizabeth Bishop and the Editors of *Life, Brazil* (New York: Time) was first published Feb. 10, 1962. MacMahon, 54, 156.

16. All references to *Brazil* in this paragraph are to pp. 26-28, except for Bishop's allusion on p. 31 to Samuel Putnam. Bishop complained that the editors of *Brazil* made many changes (see MacMahon, 54, and George Starbuck, " 'The Work!': A Conversation with Elizabeth Bishop," in Schwartz and Estes, eds., 312-13), but the passages I refer to appear in her typescript, Vassar College Library. For Putnam, from whom I quote Anchieta and Nobrega, see *Marvelous Journey: A Survey of Four Centuries of Brazilian Writing* (New York: Knopf, 1948), 3-4.

17. Vassar College Library.

18. Clarice Lispector, "The Smallest Woman in the World," trans. Elizabeth Bishop, *Kenyon Review* 26 (1964): 501.

19. Bishop, *Brazil*, 26.

20. Ian Hamilton, *Robert Lowell: A Biography* (New York: Random House, 1982), recounts Lowell's and Bishop's friendship from Lowell's perspective; David Kalstone, "Prodigal Years: Elizabeth Bishop and Robert Lowell, 1947-49," *Grand Street* 4 (1985), 170-93, describes it more closely from Bishop's perspective. Lowell's letters to Bishop dwell on his admiration for "The Armadillo," and not long after reading it he wrote Bishop very movingly about how he once had wished to marry her, and how the feeling of a lost chance had haunted him ever since (letter of Sept. 2, 1957, Vassar College Library). Hamilton (p. 135) tells of one episode when Lowell announced to friends that he and Bishop planned to marry—though he didn't mention the engagement to Bishop. She presumably refers to that incident, and possibly other protestations of love from Lowell, when she writes of hearts that come and go, though it seems unwise to limit her words to her relation with Lowell.

21. Richard Wilbur, "Elizabeth Bishop," in Schwartz and Estes, eds., 265. Penelope Laurans, "Old Correspondences: Prosodic Transformations in Elizabeth Bishop," in Schwartz and Estes, eds., 80-81, helpfully, if perhaps somewhat defensively, argues against the charge that the last stanza sounds unduly sentimental or moralistic.

22. Hamilton, pp. 233, 422-23, 425-26, where he quotes letters from Bishop to Lowell written in 1957 (after "The Armadillo," which was first published that year) and 1972. Apparently, a decade earlier, before Lowell's series of breakdowns and when her own life felt less settled, Bishop envied Lowell's fluency; see Kalstone, "Prodigal Years," passim, esp. 174-75, 177. Though the dedication to Lowell in "The Armadillo" did not appear in print until *Questions of Travel*, 1965, presumably Bishop told Lowell that in some sense she wrote the poem to him.

23. Elizabeth Bishop, *The Complete Poems* (New York: Farrar, Straus & Giroux, 1969), dust jacket.

24. Lowell's "imitations" (what he called his loose translations) were accused of "breezy plagiarism"; he more or less began and, with a few others, epitomized the rage for so-called "confessional" poetry; the prosaic style of his poems in the late fifties and early sixties, if not beyond then, was often accused of sounding "monotonous" (though not musically); and from the mid-sixties, when even many admirers think Lowell's work declined, he was routinely accused of riding his reputation with "empty mastery," "mismanaged fire," and "idiosyncratic incoherence."

25. Robert Lowell, "Skunk Hour," in *Life Studies* (New York: Farrar, Straus & Cudahy, 1959), 89-90. The poem is too long to quote here, especially as it is widely available, and as my emphasis is less on Lowell's poem itself than on its implicit interpretation of Bishop's poem. For discussions of "Skunk Hour," probably Lowell's most written-about poem, see most of the many books on Lowell, and *The Contemporary Poet as Artist and Critic: Eight Symposia*, ed. Anthony Ostroff (Boston: Little, Brown, 1964), 81-110.

26. Robert Lowell, in Ostroff, ed., 109.

27. Hamilton, 135.

28. The comparison of Arthur's coffin to cake and, later, of Arthur himself to a doll fits the poem's resemblance to Bishop's more-or-less autobiographical story "Gwendolyn" (1953), about the death of a doll-like childhood friend. The adult narrator recalls that, at the time, she thought her diabetic friend was all cakes and sugar. The story differs from the poem (1962) in that the dead child is a girl and unrelated rather than a boy and a cousin. The same story briefly mentions its narrator's cousin Billy, who with his father, Uncle Neddy, figures more prominently in another autobiographical story, "Memories of Uncle Neddy" (1977). The two stories' thick context of circumstance and their consistency across many years of composition suggest that they stick to autobiographical fact more closely than the poem, which perhaps condenses Gwendolyn and cousin Billy into Arthur, and derives Uncle Arthur at least partly from the Uncle Neddy of her prose. (His actual name was Arthur, and in what appear to be the earliest typescripts of "Memories of Uncle Neddy," housed in the Vassar College Library, she calls him Arthur or, more frequently, Artie.) For the stories, see *The Collected Prose*. On Bishop's habit of changing names in autobiographical materials, see Giroux's introduction, xx. On all these matters, see also Peter

Sanger, "Elizabeth Bishop and Nova Scotia," *Antigonish Review* 60 (1985): 22-27.

29. Quoted from the Johnson edition, published seven years before Bishop's poem (see Ch. 1, n. 2).

30. For a concise and usefully more general discussion of Dickinson's dashes, see Robert Weisbuch, *Emily Dickinson's Poetry* (Chicago: University of Chicago Press, 1975), 173-76. Bishop first read Dickinson before the Johnson edition (see n. 29). In the 1930 edition of "There's been a Death" the words are the same, but most of the capitalization and internal commas and dashes have been removed. Interestingly, though, "it" has been changed to "It."

31. We can make such comparisons without fussing over Dickinson's influence on Bishop in the narrow sense of imitation or phrase-mongering. There may be some of that, but grief and death are familiar subjects for many poets, and the abstract and most interesting possibilities of influence between these poems will remain intangible. If the comparison illumines either or both poets, then it does what we need. In any case, given "First Death in Nova Scotia," it is also interesting to recall Dickinson's poem 1149 (again I quote the Johnson edition, which gives the same words as the 1930 edition):

> I noticed People disappeared
> When but a little child—
> Supposed they visited remote
> Or settled Regions wild—
> Now know I—They both visited
> And settled Regions wild
> But did because they died
> A Fact withheld the little child—

32. See Susan Sontag, *On Photography* (New York: Farrar, Straus & Giroux, 1977), 70-71; Roland Barthes, *Camera Lucida: Reflections on Photography*, trans. Richard Howard (New York: Hill and Wang, 1981), 10-15, 92-97.

33. Helen Vendler, "Domestication, Domesticity, and the Otherworldly," in Schwartz and Estes, eds., 36, assumes that the girl herself imagines the "royal couples" have invited Arthur to join them. Her thoughtful discussion helped me reach my own somewhat different reading.

34. Whether my guess here is biographically correct hardly matters, for

it still holds true for the poem as autobiographical pretext, in which Bishop takes on the voice of a child from her own childhood's Nova Scotia who refers to its mother in a particular set of ways and in the first person. It is that child's attitude and its relation to Bishop's other work that I here discuss.

35. All these autobiographical memoirs of Bishop's early Nova Scotia childhood are in *The Collected Prose*.

36. Ernest Hemingway, "Indian Camp," *The Short Stories of Ernest Hemingway* (New York: Scribner's, 1938), 95, first collected in book form in *In Our Time*, 1925. Readers of "Indian Camp" will know that this final sentence, quoted by itself, cannot convey the force of Nick's collision with birth, death, and suicide, the drama of his mixing with the adult world (especially his father), or the pressure under which he thinks these thoughts. At Key West, Bishop was close friends with Pauline Hemingway, who sent Ernest *North & South*. As Bishop wrote to Anne Stevenson, "He wrote her he liked it, and, referring to 'the Fish,' I think, 'I wish I knew as much about it as she does.' Allowing for exaggeration to please his ex-wife—that remark has really meant more to me than any praise in the quarterlies. I knew that underneath Mr. H and I were really a lot alike." In a letter to May Swenson, Bishop refers to herself as a "sort of lady-Hemingway." Letters of Jan. 8, 1964, and Feb. 18, 1962, in the Elizabeth Bishop Papers and the May Swenson Papers, Washington University Libraries. On influence, see n. 31.

One highly plausible influence on "First Death in Nova Scotia," especially on its last stanza, is Mário de Andrade's "Improvisation of the Dead Boy," collected in *An Anthology of Twentieth-Century Brazilian Poetry*, ed. Elizabeth Bishop and Emanuel Brasil (Middletown, Conn.: Wesleyan University Press, 1972), 20-23, trans. Richard Eberhart. It begins "Dead, gently he lies in the flowers of the coffin," and ends with the poet pleading to the boy's body:

> "Depart! Depart, dead boy!
> Depart, for I no longer know you!
> Do not return nightly to beget upon my destiny
> The flare of your being and your desire to think!
>
> .   .   .   .
>
> Enormous, unbearable my peace!
>
> .   .   .   .
>
> What liberty in your oblivion!

What firmness of independence in your death!
Oh, depart, for I no longer know you!"

37. For information about Pound at St. Elizabeths I rely mainly on E. Fuller Torrey, *The Roots of Treason: Ezra Pound and the Secret of St. Elizabeths* (New York: McGraw-Hill, 1984); and Charles Olson, *Charles Olson & Ezra Pound: An Encounter at St. Elizabeths*, ed. Catherine Seelye (New York: Grossman, 1975). (I use the information Torrey has gathered, without adopting his not very well received interpretations of that information.)

38. Wherever the poem refers to Pound or another patient with the word "that," the manuscript in the Vassar College Library uses the word "who." The manuscript also shows that Bishop particularly worked over the adjectives for Pound.

39. Wehr, 23, quotes Bishop in 1966: "Going insane is very popular these days, and it frightens me to see so many young people flirting with the idea of it. They think that going crazy will turn them into better poets. That's just not true *at all!* Insanity is a terrible thing . . . a *terrible* thing! [Wehr's ellipses.] I've seen it first-hand in some of my friends, and it is not the 'poetic' sort of thing that these young people seem to think it is. John Clare did *not* write glorious poetry while he was in the asylum, I'm glad to say. . . . My students . . . have such narrow and sometimes destructive ideas about what it is to be a poet. I've been thinking lately that I really should say something to them about all of this. It's a very serious matter." Bishop referred to her poem's mix of praise and complaint in a letter of May 1, 1957, to Isabella Gardner: "I am glad you liked the Pound poem — I really couldn't tell myself whether it had conveyed my rather mixed emotions" (Elizabeth Bishop Papers, Washington University Libraries).

40. Samuel Taylor Coleridge, *Biographia Literaria*, ed. James Engell and W. Jackson Bate (Princeton, N.J.: Princeton University Press, 1983), I: 27-28n. See Ch. 1, nn. 9, 3. Curiously, Mildred J. Nash, "Elizabeth Bishop's Library: A Reminiscence," *Massachusetts Review* 24 (1983): 436, notes that in 1976 Bishop owned "an annotated copy of the Opies' *Nursery Rhyme Book,*" which she kept among her "best books." No book matches that title exactly, but the only one that comes close and that was annotated and published by 1976 includes a reference to Coleridge's poem in its annotation to "This is the house that Jack built," and appeared six years before Bishop's poem: *The Oxford Dictionary of Nursery Rhymes*, ed. Iona and Peter Opie (1951; reprint, London: Oxford University Press, 1952), 232. Bishop sent an "Oxford Nursery Rhyme Book" to May Swenson at

about the time she was writing "Visits to St. Elizabeths" (letter of Aug. 5, 1956, from Swenson in the May Swenson Papers, Washington University Libraries).

41. Elizabeth Bishop, blurb on the dust jacket for Robert Lowell, *Life Studies*.

42. Hamilton, 130.

43. *Life Studies*, 95-96; Anne Sexton, *The Complete Poems* (Boston: Houghton Mifflin, 1981), 28. "Visits to St. Elizabeths" was not published in book form until after "Ringing in the Bells," but Sexton probably saw it in *The New Yorker*. In an interview, she named Bishop as one of her favorite poets (*Hudson Review* 18 [Winter, 1965/66], reprinted in Anne Sexton, *No Evil Star: Selected Essays, Interviews, and Prose*, ed. Steven E. Colburn [Ann Arbor: University of Michigan Press, 1985], 72), and she wrote lavishly to Bishop about Bishop's influence on her (letters in Vassar College Library).

44. Ostroff, 109.

45. Quoted in *Time*, June 2, 1967, p. 68, and Schwartz and Estes, eds., p. 303. Wehr, p. 327, quotes Bishop in 1966: "I *hate* confessional poetry."

Chapter Four

1. David Kalstone, "Prodigal Years: Elizabeth Bishop and Robert Lowell, 1947-49," *Grand Street* 4 (1985): 178.

2. Walt Whitman, *Leaves of Grass*, ed. Sculley Bradley and Harold W. Blodgett (New York: New York University Press, 1965), 328, 330.

3. Marianne Moore, "Rigorists," in *The Complete Poems of Marianne Moore* (New York: Macmillan, 1981), 96, 276. Four concurrently written, overlapping discussions compare Moore and Bishop. Lynn Keller, "Words Worth a Thousand Postcards: The Bishop/Moore Correspondence," *American Literature* 55 (Fall, 1983): 405-29, especially studies the two poets' friendship. Bonnie Costello, "Marianne Moore and Elizabeth Bishop: Friendship and Influence," *Twentieth Century Literature* 30 (1984): 130-49, emphasizes the two kinds of poetry they produced. Denis Donoghue, *Connoisseurs of Chaos: Ideas of Order in Modern American Poetry*, 2nd ed. (New York: Columbia University Press, 1984), 275-76, objects to the idea that Moore and Bishop have much in common. And David Kalstone, "Trial Balances: Elizabeth Bishop and Marianne Moore," in *Coming to Light: American Women Poets in the Twentieth Century*, ed. Diane Wood Middlebrook and Marilyn Yalom (Ann Arbor: University of Michigan Press,

1985), concentrates on Moore's role in the emergence of Bishop's own manner.

4. Elizabeth Bishop, "As We Like It," in *Quarterly Review of Literature* 4 (1948): 134, quoting "leathern coat" from a passage she finds naively anthropomorphic in Shakespeare's *As You Like It*, II.ii

5. J. D. McClatchy, "Some Notes on 'One Art,'" *Field* 31 (Fall, 1984): 39.

6. Her preoccupation with scale appears even in her high school magazine, where she wrote that "There is always something strangely fascinating for us in the idea of things planned on a different scale from our own mortal inches and feet," quoted from Elizabeth Bishop, "Giant Weather," *The Blue Pencil* 12 (Dec., 1928): 4. Bishop's papers at the Vassar College Library show her pondering the material for "12 O'Clock News" through over forty years of assorted drafts.

7. Crusoe's unbelief here differs a good deal from the reaffirmation of belief in Defoe's Crusoe. Bishop complained in an interview that Defoe's book "was so moral. All that Christianity. So I think I wanted to re-see it with all that left out." George Starbuck, " 'The Work!': A Conversation with Elizabeth Bishop," in *Elizabeth Bishop and Her Art*, ed. Lloyd Schwartz and Sybil P. Estes (Ann Arbor: University of Michigan Press, 1983), 319. Her poem sounds closer to the adult's retrospective relativism in Carlos Drummond de Andrade's "Infancy," which Bishop, who translated it, would surely have in mind. It ends, in her translation, with the speaker recollecting "And I didn't know that my story / was prettier than that of Robinson Crusoe." She also would think of William Cowper's "The Castaway," a poem she wrote Anne Stevenson that she had a weakness for (letter of Jan. 8, 1964, to Stevenson in the Elizabeth Bishop Papers, Washington University Libraries). That poem might also remind her of Cowper's "Verses supposed to be written by Alexander Selkirk during his Solitary Abode in the Island of Juan Fernandez," especially since Selkirk was Defoe's model for Crusoe.

8. Robert Lowell, *Lord Weary's Castle* (New York: Harcourt, Brace, Jovanovich, 1946), 61.

9. Bishop names the Ten Thousand Islands (off the southwest coast of Florida) and Aruba as among her sources for Crusoe's island. Starbuck, 317, 319. Keller, "Words Worth a Thousand Postcards," 410-14, stresses Bishop's preoccupation with description of flora and fauna in her letters to Marianne Moore. That same preoccupation, of course, shows throughout her poetry and prose.

10. *The Poems of Emily Dickinson*, ed. Thomas H. Johnson (Cambridge, Mass.: Harvard University Press, 1955), poem 280.

11. Elizabeth Bishop, "Flannery O'Connor, 1925-1964," *The New York Review of Books*, Oct. 8, 1964, 21. Bishop began a friendship with O'Connor by writing her (Flannery O'Connor, *The Habit of Being*, ed. Sally Fitzgerald [New York: Random House, 1979], 197-98, 248). She often referred to her admiration for O'Connor, and praised some of her stories — including "Rev-elation" — "as just about the best American stories I have ever read" (letter of May 2, 1965, to May Swenson in the May Swenson Papers, Washington University Libraries).

12. William Carlos Williams, *Paterson* (New York: New Directions, 1963), Book I, Part I, 13-14. The familiarity of such materials as a feature of *National Geographic* shows the more when we consider that no such pictures actually appear in the February 1918 issue (vol. 33, which does include Robert F. Griggs, "The Valley of Ten Thousand Smokes: An Account of the Discovery and Exploration of the Most Wonderful Volcanic Region in the World," 115-69). Consciously or not, Bishop simply made up the pictures of naked women, partly from what she would have seen in any number of other issues, and partly, it appears, from the autobiography of Osa Johnson, unforgettably titled *I Married Adventure* (New York: J. B. Lippincott, 1940); see Lee Edelman, "The Geography of Gender: Elizabeth Bishop's 'In the Waiting Room,' " *Contemporary Literature* 26 (1985): 179-96. Edelman, in his resourceful discovery and discussion of Johnson's book, does not note that one picture in her book fits with striking aptness the general pattern described in Bishop's poem. It shows Osa Johnson standing among a group of black, bare-breasted Pygmies, almost all women, and with very uncomfortable expressions on their faces as they uncertainly look off to the side of the camera. Meanwhile, blithely unconcerned with her hosts' uneasiness, the white and fully-dressed Osa Johnson cradles one Pygmy woman like a baby in her arms and grins right into the lens. The caption says: "Five-foot Osa lifts a Pygmy, the mother of five children" (illustration facing p. 331). The picture thus perfectly captures the pre-sumptions of difference and superiority that Bishop's poem calls into ques-tion. "The Country Mouse," her earlier (1961) prose account of the episode in the dentist's office, centers on the same crisis of suddenly realized identity, but says nothing about femininity or what was in the magazine. In that earlier version, the crisis seems tipped off — perhaps in part by the self-consciousness of observing and being observed in the waiting room — but

otherwise simply by the date on the magazine cover and its reminder of her approaching birthday. See Elizabeth Bishop, *The Collected Prose*, ed. Robert Giroux (New York: Farrar, Straus & Giroux, 1984), 32-33.

13. "The Country Mouse," 33.

14. Flannery O'Connor, "Revelation," in *The Complete Stories* (New York: Farrar, Straus & Giroux, 1971), 507.

15. O'Connor, *The Habit of Being*, 117, 124. Quotations from "A Temple of the Holy Ghost" are from *The Complete Stories*, 236-48.

16. "Gwendolyn," in Bishop, *The Collected Prose*, 226.

17. Elizabeth Bishop, "The Pencil Sharpener," *The Blue Pencil* 13 (Dec., 1929): 4.

18. "The Country Mouse"; see n. 12.

19. Letter to May Swenson in the May Swenson Papers, Washington University Libraries; David Kalstone, "Prodigal Years: Elizabeth Bishop and Robert Lowell, 1947-49," p. 180.

20. Letter to May Swenson in the May Swenson Papers, Washington University Libraries.

21. She uses the same sentence in "The Country Mouse," p. 26.

Index

A Note on the Author

Robert Dale Parker teaches English at the University of Illinois at Urbana-Champaign. His first book, also published by the University of Illinois Press, was *Faulkner and the Novelistic Imagination* (1985).